TAG, YOU'RE IT!!!

The Secret Game that is Destroying Your Marriage

By

Glenn Pickering, MDiv, PhD

Unless otherwise indicated, all Scripture quotations are taken from the Holy Bible, Revised Standard Version.

Any emphasis within Scripture quotations are the author's own.

TAG, YOU'RE IT!!!
The Secret Game that is Destroying Your Marriage
ISBN: 0-9776294-0-6

Printed in the United States of America

Beginning Now Media
6542 Regency Lane
Suite 205
Eden Prairie, MN 55344
www.BeginningNowMinistries.org

2 3 4 5 6 7 8 9 10 / 09 08 07 06

Contents

An Introduction to TAG

I call TAG a game but its impact upon your marriage is no game.

Unless you quit playing, right now, the game will destroy your relationship.

Yes, that's right–you are already playing TAG.

Every petty argument you have, every time you think you need to be "right," every time you feel that you are not in love, every time you insist on being in control, every time you leave in a huff, and every time that you are afraid to tell your truth, you are playing the game.

And every time you play, you put one more brick in the wall.

That's why I say that if you don't stop playing, you will destroy your marriage. Because once that wall gets thick enough, the love stops flowing.

And then it's over.

You might stay together. But the marriage will be over.

Not because you picked the wrong person. Because you played TAG.

Luckily, our God is a God of transformation. With His help, you can create a radically different kind of marriage.

Starting right now.

As soon as you learn how to quit playing TAG, the miracle of love will reappear. Intimacy will flourish, your family will thrive, and love will abound.

I want those miracles for you.

So let's get started.

Acknowledgments

I wish to thank:

My beloved wife, Gwen, who has the courage to learn and grow with me, every day.

My amazing daughter, Rachel, who insures that I never take myself too seriously.

Pete Larson, at Bethany Press, who initiated this entire process.

God, who would not let me sleep until I wrote this book.

CHAPTER 1:

Living the Game

As our story opens, it is very early in the morning and Joe is getting ready to leave for work. He is a computer engineer by trade and has been putting in many long hours these past few months on a major project that is integral to the success of his company.

He enters the kitchen, where his wife, Elizabeth, is preparing breakfast for their 9-year-old daughter, Sabrina, and 7-year-old daughter, Sandi. Elizabeth is a former teacher, a stay-at-home mom, and an active volunteer in the community and at church.

Joe began by saying, "Honey, I can't find this week's bills."

Elizabeth replied, "You're the grouch who insisted that the bills not be put on his desk."

"All I said was I needed my desk to be less cluttered and more organized. I never said we shouldn't put the mail there," responded Joe defensively.

"You should have organized your desk then," Elizabeth responded.

You know that I've been really busy lately," Joe explained.

Elizabeth said sharply, "I'm not the one who brings in the mail anyway. You know that."

"Did Sabrina bring it in?" asked Joe in a placating tone.

"Sabrina always brings it in," responded Elizabeth curtly.

"Why are you so upset with me? I didn't do anything wrong."

Elizabeth's voice rose. "I'm not upset. I just don't like getting blamed for things that aren't my fault."

"I was just asking where the bills are so we don't lose them," Joe explained.

Elizabeth was indignant. "I've never lost a bill in my life."

"Well, we easily could if we don't come up with a better system," Joe pointed out.

"I don't want to talk about this anymore. Have a good day at work," said Elizabeth, in a voice devoid of emotion.

Later as Elizabeth was driving to a luncheon gathering with four of her friends, she was still upset and confused. Why was Joe always picking on her? Why wasn't anything ever good enough for him? And when had she become so defensive and so bitter?

Elizabeth was still visibly upset as she sat in the restaurant with her friends.

"What's wrong?" asked her old college friend Joan. "I've never seen you like this before. You look like you're sad and like you could kill somebody at the same time."

"It's true that I am very upset and mixed up. Joe and I had a mean-spirited argument before he left today—one of those arguments where he acts as though he's Mister Perfect."

Joan looked at her skeptically. "You're this upset just because you had an argument?"

"No," Elizabeth replied. "I'm upset and confused because we have so many arguments these days. I'm scared because I can feel us drifting apart."

Barb interjected, "I knew you guys were having problems but I didn't know it was so serious."

Elizabeth nodded. "Yes, it's serious. I really am scared. And what scares me the most is the fact that even though I can feel us drifting apart, I don't seem to care. In fact, I'm starting to forget why I ever liked Joe in the first place. He seems so distant and so hard to love these days. Sometimes I wonder if it weren't for the kids, if I'd ever spend another minute with him."

"I know what you mean," Barb concurred. "Sometimes I look at Harry across the breakfast table and wonder, 'Am I only sitting here because I'm too lazy or too scared to leave?' And I'm afraid of the answer."

"Do you ever tell Harry that you have doubts about the relationship?" Elizabeth wondered.

Barb snorted. "The last time I told Harry I wanted us to be closer, he said we just needed to have sex more often."

Elizabeth nodded sadly. "Well, all I know for sure is that I just don't feel the same connection to Joe anymore. I still love him, I think, but I'm not in love with him. Is that terrible?"

At this point, her friend Anita joined the conversation. "Elizabeth, you are such a romantic. Of course you don't feel 'in love' anymore–that feeling NEVER lasts. Welcome to the real world."

Barb agreed. "Yeah, the kids come along, life gets busy, and love fades. That's just the way it is. Everybody says so."

Anita continued. "You should just be glad you still have a husband. He's nice to the neighbors and he's great with the kids, isn't he? That's a lot more than most women can say."

Elizabeth shook her head vehemently and asked, "Are you saying that I should tolerate my current situation, even though Joe is controlling, throws tantrums like a two-year-old, and is so critical of me?"

Anita put her hand gently on Elizabeth's arm. "No, I'm just saying that fairy tales aren't real. You're not Cinderella, Joe is not the shining knight on the white horse, and being in love is just a story they tell in the movies."

Elizabeth looked puzzled. "So, Anita, you don't think that the feeling of being in love is important?"

"I'm saying it can't possibly be important because it isn't even real."

Elizabeth's shoulders slumped. "So I should just make the best of it?"

Anita put her palms up. "What other choice do you have?"

Joan shook her head vigorously. "I totally disagree with you, Anita. I think that being in love is terribly important. No woman should stay in a relationship if she no longer feels loved and adored."

"What are you saying?" Elizabeth asked.

Joan continued. "Well, you obviously don't feel cherished anymore. Plus, you no longer respect Joe. You're not in love, you argue all the time now, and it seems as though you're only staying for the kids. Maybe you just need to admit that it's time to end it."

Elizabeth reluctantly agreed. "All of the things that you said are true. But does that really mean that it has to be over?"

Joan shrugged her shoulders. "Honey, once the love is gone, it's already over."

Elizabeth started crying.

Joan immediately wished that she had not spoken so harshly. "I'm sorry. I shouldn't have been so blunt. All I know is that it seems like the two of you are too far gone for there to be any hope."

"You might be right," Elizabeth acknowledged. "There is not a lot left between us. In fact, at this point it is hard for me to even be in the same room as Joe. Everything he does drives me away. It's like he is constantly trying to find new ways to irritate me. Many times, all I can do is leave the room."

Barb brightened and said, "You know, maybe it would be better to move on. There's a cute guy at work I'd love to introduce you to–the two of you would be perfect for each other. Do you want his number?"

Elizabeth just shook her head and numbly dropped out of the conversation.

Later, as she left the restaurant, Elizabeth felt unsettled and restless. She got into her car, started to put the key in the ignition, then stopped and laid the key in her lap. She closed her eyes and prayerfully asked God to reveal to her the cause of her unhappiness. In that quiet moment, she came to see that she was troubled for two reasons.

First, she felt that she had somehow betrayed Joe. Yes, it was true they had been drifting apart for quite some time but he wasn't the bad guy she had made him out to be. In her anger and disappointment she had made him sound like one of those childish, uncaring slobs they show on TV and he simply wasn't like that. He loved the children, was active in the church, took care of the house, paid the bills, and attended endless PTA meetings without complaint. And yet, with her friends, she had made him sound terrible. What was wrong with her?

Second, the advice she had received from her friends had left her feeling paralyzed–unsure of how to proceed. Should she stay and just stick it out, even though she was terribly unhappy? Or should she admit that her love had died and find a new and exciting lover, someone who would make her forget all about Joe? Neither solution seemed right to Elizabeth, yet she could see no other realistic answers. And it was this lack of positive options that was making her feeling so restless.

Suddenly, she realized that her best friend, Linda, had not actually said anything to her during lunch. That was unusual—Linda was her closest Christian friend and the one whose advice was invariably helpful. Why had she failed to speak up?

That evening, after Joe and the kids had gone to bed, Elizabeth called Linda.

"I wanted to talk with you about the conversation at lunch. I noticed that you didn't say anything at all. I wondered what you were thinking."

After a pause, Linda replied, "Well, I wasn't sure what to say, partly because of the seriousness of the situation and partly because I so totally disagreed with everyone else."

"What do you mean?" Elizabeth wondered.

Linda responded, "I don't think you should simply tolerate a bad marriage. To passively continue to live the way you have been living would be a waste of your life."

Elizabeth grinned. "Linda, that's what I've always loved about you–you're so subtle."

"Well, I just don't want you to make the same mistake as the guy in the Matthew 25 story of the talents—the one who basically chose to do nothing with his life because he was afraid to make a change—afraid to use the talents God gave him."

"I never thought about it like that. You're right. It was displeasing to God that the man never even tried to use the talents he had been given. I wouldn't want that to be me. I don't want to just bury my head in the sand and pretend everything is okay."

Linda simply continued. "But I don't think it makes any sense to simply leave your marriage either. The two of you have a lot invested in that relationship and in that family. You wouldn't want to just throw that away."

Elizabeth concurred. "I've often had that same thought–all those years down the drain."

Linda hesitated, then said, "Plus, I know you felt strongly that God had led you to Joe. If He chose Joe for you then, how can he be the wrong guy for you now?"

Elizabeth was quiet a long time. "I'm so lost—I don't know what to do. You're right, I can't stay where I am and it feels wrong to leave."

Linda spoke gently, "I think you may be overlooking an obvious third choice."

"What do you mean?"

Linda asked, "Have you considered fighting for the relationship?"

"Are you kidding? We fight all the time!" exclaimed Elizabeth.

"Yes, but right now you each only fight for yourselves. There is no one who is fighting for the relationship," Linda pointed out.

"Ouch! Okay, that's true. How do we do that 'fighting for the relationship' thing you're talking about?" Elizabeth wondered.

"I think you're going to need help in order to learn that."

Elizabeth wrinkled her brow. "What sort of help?"

Linda responded, "You need to go see a marriage counselor—someone who helps people to make their relationships richer and stronger."

"I don't know," Elizabeth said doubtfully. "Does that ever really work? Those people always seem goofy when they show them on TV."

"I know what you mean," replied Linda. "But there have to be people out there who are good at it–people who really do know what they're doing."

Elizabeth brightened at the thought. "You're right; there must be some really good relationship experts out there. Do you know any?"

Linda shook her head. "No, but it shouldn't be that hard to locate one. We can start doing some research together."

"Okay. I would like that a lot."

When Elizabeth went to bed that night, she felt a faint glimmer of hope. Maybe there was someone who could help them. If there was, she would not rest until she found that person. Linda was right—her marriage and her family were simply too important to quit without a fight! She would talk to Joe when he got home from work tomorrow.

The next morning, Joe left the house at 6 a.m. to meet for breakfast with his Men of Faith accountability group.

He started by saying, "As you know, I just started with the group a little while ago and so far I've mostly just listened. But today I really need feedback."

"What's the matter?" John asked sympathetically.

Joe replied, "Elizabeth and I are having real problems and I don't know what to do."

"What kind of problems?" John wondered.

Joe shrugged. "I know it sounds like a cliché, but we just can't seem to communicate."

John looked confused. "I don't understand. You always speak so clearly here."

"Yeah," added Mark. "I don't get it either. Whenever I talk with either of you at church you always seem to be so articulate. How could there be a communication problem?"

Joe shrugged his shoulders. "I honestly don't know what's happening. When I try to talk to Elizabeth, it's as if there's a wall there."

"Is there another guy?" Mark wondered.

"Elizabeth has always been so serious about our marriage and about her faith that I can't believe she would do that," Joe said, shaking his head. "It's not like her. But then, this isn't like her either."

"What do you mean?" asked Mark.

Joe replied, "She always used to be interested in me and in the things I would talk to her about. But now she doesn't really listen to anything I say. When I try to start a conversation, instead of listening, she either tells me what to do, lashes out, or just shuts down. It's like she doesn't actually want to connect with me. And so now we don't talk at all."

Mark looked shocked. "Not ever?"

Joe modified his statement a bit. "Well, hardly ever. And when we do talk, it seems like it always leads to an argument."

Steve jumped in. "What do you argue about?"

Joe paused, then said, "You know, I can't even tell you. All I know for sure is that we argue about the dumbest stuff. It's like we can't even speak to each other for more than a minute without having it turn into another fight."

"Do those fights ever help to clear the air?" Steve asked.

Joe shook his head. "No, that's the worst part. We have a terrible argument and when it's over, I realize that we didn't resolve anything. In fact, after its over, I can hardly remember what we were fighting about or why we started fighting in the first place. It all seems so pointless."

"Sounds awful," said Steve. "What are you going to do?"

"Well, for a long time I tried to avoid all of the topics that I thought would start a fight. But almost anything can. That's why I've pretty much quit talking to her altogether," Joe explained.

John noted, "You've been working a lot lately."

Joe hung his head and acknowledged, "I know it sounds bad, but I have to admit that lately I have been finding lots of ways to avoid spending time with my own wife. I admit that it doesn't make things any better in the long run, but it does make things easier for the short term."

"Sounds pretty empty," responded John, without condemnation. "It sounds like the arguments and the avoidance have taken all the romance out of your marriage."

"Yeah," Joe confirmed, "it's as though we're just roommates now, instead of husband and wife."

Mark glumly added, "That's how my brother described his marriage, too, just before he got divorced."

Steve turned toward Joe and said, "Maybe it's over. Have you ever thought about that?"

Joe replied, "Although I hate to admit it, I think about that pretty often. But then I think about the kids and it makes me sick to think that I wouldn't be able to see them every day and to tuck them into bed each night."

There were nods all around the table.

Mark spoke up, "Yeah, that would be awful."

Joe continued, "Besides, I made a vow. I promised God and Elizabeth that I wouldn't bail just because we hit a hard stretch. How could I ever face myself knowing that I quit?"

"It's a tough spot to be in," Steve responded.

Joe agreed passionately. "What I have now is awful and leaving would be worse. I feel totally paralyzed. It's SO frustrating."

"I think you need to go see Dr. Richard Scott," said John, in a voice that was both quiet and confident.

"Who is Dr. Richard Scott?"

"He's a Christian psychologist who is also a Certified Marriage Educator—a person who specializes in relational transformation."

Joe immediately got defensive. "What would a psychologist be able to do for us? It's not like we're crazy, you know. We just don't communicate very well with each other."

John continued in the same tone of voice. "Karen and I saw Dr. Scott a few years ago and he helped us to totally re-create our marriage."

Joe was truly surprised. "You guys needed help? I don't believe that."

John nodded. "It's true that things are going incredibly well for Karen and me. But there was a time, before you joined this group, when we experienced many of the same problems you were just talking about: the fighting, the silence, the avoidance, and the persistent thoughts of divorce. In fact, without his help we probably would have gotten divorced. We would have been one of those awful statistics you're always reading about."

Joe responded sarcastically, as if he was almost afraid to believe it. "How did he help you? Did he wave a magic wand, or something?"

John just smiled. "No, he taught us lots of helpful things, but mostly he taught us how to quit playing a game he calls TAG–a game I think you and Elizabeth now play pretty much all of the time."

"What in the world is TAG?" Joe asked, with a touch of belligerence still in his voice.

"I'll let him explain that to you and Elizabeth. I will tell you, though, that the moment you quit playing TAG, your marriage will improve instantly. Dr. Scott can teach you how to drop all of your useless arguments and instead develop a truly Christian marriage—one that is fun, joyful, powerful, and passionate. Isn't that what you want?"

"Yes," said Joe, "I want that so badly I am afraid to even hope for it."

John responded gently, "I know what you mean; that's how I felt too."

"What exactly should I say to Elizabeth?" Joe asked nervously.

"Don't worry about your exact words. Just take a prayerful moment, ask God to help you to remember just how lucky you are to even know Elizabeth, and then lovingly invite her to go see Dr. Scott with you."

Joe still hesitated. "What if she won't go?"

John shook his head. "Joe, give Elizabeth a little credit. She isn't blind. She sees the same problems you do. And she wants a real Christian marriage just as badly as you do. In fact, she's probably wishing right now that you would take the lead and get the two of you moving in the right direction. Besides, if she has any questions she can call Karen–my honey loves to talk about TAG and about the work that Dr. Scott does with couples."

"Okay," Joe agreed, smiling for the first time. "I'll talk with Elizabeth tonight."

John nodded his approval. "Great! If it's okay with you guys, let's close with a word of prayer for our brother, that he may receive the guidance, the clarity, and the strength he needs."

Everyone concurred and prayed that Joe might indeed be made ready for the journey.

CHAPTER 2:

Learning the Game

"Hello. You must be Joe and Elizabeth."

Joe replied, "Yes. It's good to meet you, Dr. Scott," while Elizabeth simply nodded her agreement.

"Thanks," responded Dr. Scott. "How can I be of help to you?"

"Well, we're not sure," said Joe. "Our friends John and Karen recommended that we see you."

"Why did they recommend that?" Dr. Scott wondered.

"They say we frequently play a game that you call TAG and that the game is destroying our marriage," explained Joe. "I don't know if the part about our playing the game is true but I know that they are right about one thing–our marriage is really suffering."

Dr. Scott nodded. "In just a minute I'll tell you a little bit about TAG and then you can tell me if you have indeed been playing the game. But first let me get you each a journal and pen so you can take careful notes during our sessions. That way you can review our sessions after each meeting, and after our first few meetings we can evaluate our progress."

"Okay."

After making sure that Joe and Elizabeth had the necessary materials, Dr. Scott began. "Our faith makes it clear just how terribly important it is for us to be in right relationship. Our scriptures command us to love one another and state that the greatest commandment is to be in right relationship with God and with each other. Our God calls us not into a list of rules or even into a religion but into a holy and transforming relationship. And our churches are meant to be a sacred community—an experience of living rightly with one another."

Elizabeth smiled. "Dr. Scott, I have never thought of our faith in exactly that way, but you're right, it is completely about being in right relationship."

"Wow!" said Joe. "We both have been a long way from being in right relationship. No wonder our faith lives have also been suffering."

Dr. Scott nodded. "When you see clearly the critical importance of being in right relationship, you start to understand why Jesus says in Mathew 5 that we ought not even approach the altar as long as there is a rift between us and a brother or sister. We cannot even worship with a clean heart as long as we continue in wrong relationship.

So the scriptures are clear. As Christians, we simply cannot afford to be in a destructive relationship—especially a bad marriage. We are mandated to seek reconciliation. So if we are struggling in a relationship, getting help is not a luxury—it's a commandment!"

Joe looked a bit taken back, then said, "I was scared to come today. Now I am really pleased we are here. I can see that we were called to do this."

Elizabeth teared up a bit, then remarked, "For the first time in a long time I feel as though we have a sense of purpose."

Dr. Scott smiled and said, "Well, let's get started on that purpose then.

"Everything that goes wrong with our life is caused by our being in wrong relationship with someone. And every form of wrong relationship is caused by our playing the game I call TAG."

Elizabeth raised her eyebrows. "That's a big statement."

"Yes, but it's also an accurate one, as you will find out. That's why it is so terribly important for every person, especially every Christian, to understand the game."

"I'm all ears," Joe said.

Dr. Scott smiled. "I have to start by giving you a little background. I came to understand, quite some time ago, that Rule #1 in any abusive or addictive family is this: If I can prove that I'm right and you're wrong, I can be as mean to you as I want. To which the abusive person would add, 'and it's your fault that I am acting this way. I am not a bad or cruel person–I am just giving you what you deserve, stupid. You messed up and you therefore deserve to be treated harshly.' That's Rule #1."

Elizabeth interrupted to ask, "Dr. Scott, are you saying that Joe and I are abusive people?"

"No, not at all," replied Dr. Scott, reassuringly. "Bear with me and I promise that it will all make sense to you in just a minute."

"Thanks–I'm sorry I interrupted."

Dr. Scott waved off her apology. "No problem. Anyway, once I understood Rule #1, I also came to understand that there were three very specific behaviors that always occurred as a result of this rule—three consistent corollaries to Rule #1. If you were to put an abusive or addictive family in a glass house and just observe them for a while, like a scientist observing nature, you would notice these three patterns of behavior.

"First you would notice that there were NO real conversations in this family–no intimate moments in which people listened carefully to and connected deeply with one another. Instead, you would see that every comment triggered a knee-jerk defensive reaction, every interaction was characterized by an argumentative tone, and every conversation ended with the family members feeling attacked and misunderstood.

"In other words, you would notice that every interaction was really just an argument. That's the first corollary to Rule #1–everything leads to an argument."

"That's us!" exclaimed Joe. "Those are almost exactly the words I used when I described our marriage to the Men of Faith—my men's accountability group."

"Yes," agreed Elizabeth, "we do seem to argue about everything lately."

Dr. Scott turned to her and replied, "Okay, then perhaps we are indeed on the right track."

Joe nodded. "Please keep going, Dr. Scott."

"The second thing you would notice about the abusive or addictive family in that glass house–the second corollary–follows directly after the first. Once you had come to understand that every interaction led to an argument, you would start paying closer attention to the content of those arguments. And you would soon realize that not only does every conversation turn into an argument, it turns into the SAME argument, over and over again–an argument, it would seem, about who was right. No matter the topic, no matter the people involved, and no matter the setting, the arguments would all follow that same pattern."

Elizabeth looked thoughtful. "It's true that our arguments do seem to follow some sort of a pattern–and not a good pattern either. They all lead to the same dead end."

Joe grimaced. "Elizabeth is right. I don't know exactly what the pattern is, but I do know that I often feel like, 'Oh no, here we go again.' I hate that feeling. It gives me a knot in my stomach."

Dr. Scott nodded. "It sounds like the two of you have already discovered the second corollary–that not only does every conversation lead to an argument, it leads to the same destructive argument, over and over again. And I think if you stopped to analyze the content of those arguments, you would notice that each one seemed to degenerate into a 'me versus you' power struggle—a repetitive argument about who was right."

Elizabeth nodded vigorously. "I'm sure you're right, doctor. In fact, that's how it always was in the family I grew up in, too. There were lots of loud arguments, with everyone always acting like they needed to be right."

Dr. Scott asked her, "How did you deal with that?"

Elizabeth responded, "There were times when I got pretty loud myself. But mostly I dealt with their constant conflict by just taking care of things myself, without saying anything to anyone else. That way no one could argue with me as to whether I was doing things 'the right way' or not."

Dr. Scott took note, then said, "Thank you, Elizabeth; those are good examples of an active and a passive response to TAG. Now, here's the real key to the game. If you continued to observe that abusive or addictive family, you would begin to pay explicit attention to that one argument the family kept having. And if you paid careful attention, you would come to understand that the argument was NOT about who was RIGHT. You would discover the third corollary–that every argument was actually an argument about who was NOT WRONG!"

Joe looked puzzled. "Dr. Scott, I don't want to be critical, but isn't that the same thing?"

"No, Joe, it isn't. You see, if I was a member of that six-person abusive family, I would never be arguing that I was the one person out of those six who was right. I would be desperately arguing that I was one of the five people who were NOT WRONG. Because, remember, the person who turns out to be wrong is going to be treated terribly by all the rest of us. That's Rule #1!"

Joe's eyes lit up. "Oh, I get it. They're just trying to avoid being the bad one, the stupid one, or the one who messed up."

Dr. Scott smiled broadly. "Exactly. In this family, it is not important to be right. But it is terribly important not to be wrong. And so each person in that family strives constantly not to be wrong–not to be the bad one."

"That makes perfect sense to me now," said Joe.

"Great. Elizabeth, does it make sense to you too?"

"Yes," she responded. "You're saying that the people in my family were not actually trying to be right all of the time. It's just that they were terribly afraid of being wrong."

"Precisely," agreed Dr. Scott. "Now perhaps you can see why I call this TAG–because it's just like the game of Tag we used to play when we were kids."

"In what way?" wondered Elizabeth.

Dr. Scott prompted her by saying, "Think about it–what was the goal of that childhood game of tag?"

"To not be IT!" she exclaimed.

Dr. Scott smiled at her exuberance. "Right–to not be IT. There was nothing of a positive nature that we were trying to accomplish, no points we were trying to score, and no way to WIN the game. At any given moment, all we were trying to do was to NOT be IT."

"So that's what the members of that abusive or addictive family are trying to do–they are always trying to not be IT," she said, testing her understanding.

"Exactly," Dr. Scott confirmed. "Every minute of every day they are trying not to be IT. In other words, they are constantly playing TAG–the hurtful adult version of the innocent game of Tag that we played when we were kids."

Joe looked puzzled. "That's an interesting concept, doctor, but what has that got to do with our marriage?"

Dr. Scott turned to face Joe directly. "Good question. This is where it starts to get really interesting. As it turns out, we all play TAG at least some of the time."

"Everyone?" Joe asked, skeptically.

Dr. Scott nodded. "Yes, everyone. In fact, there are only three ways to interact: we can have factual conversations, we can have intimate conversations, or we can play TAG. That means that unless you and the other person are either exchanging information or getting to know each other better, you are indeed playing TAG."

"Wow, so TAG must happen a lot," Joe realized.

"Yes," affirmed Dr. Scott. "Once you understand TAG and can recognize it when you see it, you will be stunned to realize how incredibly often the game is played."

Joe nodded. "I'm beginning to believe you. I've often said that my dad was too critical of me. Really, he was just playing TAG."

"Right!" exclaimed Dr. Scott. "And you were almost always IT. And that sick feeling you get in your stomach when you and Elizabeth play TAG is how it feels to be IT."

A light bulb went off for Joe. "That explains a lot. I get sick to my stomach now, just like I did when I was a kid, because we are playing TAG with each other , just like dad did with me. And so now I'm avoiding Elizabeth, just like I avoided him."

Dr. Scott was impressed. "I'm glad the concept is already being so helpful to you."

Joe looked puzzled. "So, since everyone plays TAG, just like that abusive or addictive family, how can you tell the difference between a family that's abusive and one that isn't? Are you saying that Elizabeth and I are abusive to each other?"

"Those are good questions," responded Dr. Scott. "Like everything else in life, it's a matter of degree. For me, it comes down to these three guidelines: abusive and addictive families play TAG 24/7, they refuse to acknowledge the game's impact upon their family, and even when you show them a better way to interact, they continue in their destructive ways. The rest of us, on the other hand, only play TAG some of the time, we get alarmed when we realize the effect it is having on our relationships, and we are willing to learn a different way of interacting once we understand that we have a choice."

Joe brightened. "So we do have a choice?"

Dr. Scott replied confidently, "Oh, sure, you can start being different today."

"Doctor, I would dearly love to believe that statement. But how can it be true? If it took Elizabeth and me 15 years of marriage to get this messed up, won't it take us years to get it right?"

Dr. Scott shook his head vigorously. "Joe, if you are willing to learn what I teach you and practice the assignments I give you, you will see a difference within a week."

"A week?" Joe replied, in obvious disbelief.

"A week," repeated Dr. Scott. "And within eight to ten weeks the two of you will have a radically different marriage than you do right now–one that is truly intimate and powerfully loving."

Joe smiled. "If that's true, doctor, you've got yourself a client."

Dr. Scott noticed that Elizabeth seemed to have withdrawn from the conversation. He turned to her and asked, "What are you thinking?"

"Well, I was actually thinking about three things. They all sound kind of bad, though, so I don't want to say them out loud."

Dr. Scott smiled. "Go ahead. I think I can safely promise that your questions won't shock or upset me."

Elizabeth took a deep breath and launched into her concerns. "Okay, the first thing I was wondering about was this: my friend Joan said that maybe it was too late, that there had been too much damage done and we should just admit that the marriage was over. How can I tell if it's too late?"

"That's an easy one," replied Dr. Scott. "It's never too late."

"What?" asked an incredulous Elizabeth.

"There's no such thing," asserted Dr. Scott.

"How can that be true?" Elizabeth asked, almost belligerently.

Dr. Scott just smiled at her challenging tone and said, "Any two people whose hearts are open to God's leading, who choose to learn the skills I teach them, and who follow through on the assignments I give them will soon experience true intimacy. Eventually, they will develop the sort of God-led relationship that will be a source of inspiration to all those around them."

"What if the two of you have made some truly awful mistakes in the past?" asked Elizabeth.

"That's not an 'if.' Of course you have," replied Dr. Scott. "And I'm here to tell you, it simply doesn't matter. Just watch—as soon as the two of you begin to develop the kind of loving soul-mate marriage that you have always wanted, you won't even care about your past mistakes. They will be irrelevant to you."

"Wow, so the past doesn't matter," Elizabeth responded, with a question remaining in her voice.

"Not in the least. Our God is a God of transformation. The instant we ask Him to help us change, the transformational process begins. And once it begins we quickly realize that the past in no way limits His ability to mold us and to lead us into right relationship."

"Then why would my friend Joan say that my relationship was over and that I should leave Joe?"

Dr. Scott grimaced. "I notice that people are always advising others to do what they themselves have always done, even though that path has never actually worked for them. I'm thinking of writing a book entitled, 'Why Your Friends Are Always Wrong.' What do you think?"

Elizabeth smiled broadly. "Karen didn't tell us that you were so funny."

Dr. Scott smiled in return. "Sometimes the truth is the funniest thing of all. Let me ask you this–do Joan's relationships ever work out?"

"No, she keeps leaving the guy she's with as soon as their relationship hits a wall."

Dr. Scott said, "Yes, that is what I expected to hear. So if you took her advice, that would be your life too. Is that what you want?"

"Not in the least," responded Elizabeth, definitely.

"So, that's clear—she can be your friend, but she can't be your relationship advisor."

"Well, then what should a couple do if they hit the wall?" Elizabeth wondered.

Dr. Scot replied, "Again, that's not an 'if,' that's a 'when.' In every meaningful long-term relationship there will be four, or five, or six times when the two of you stand at a crossroad. And at each of those crossroads, you will face a decision—you can either choose to leave the relationship or to be transformed. If you always choose the first option, you never learn anything, which means that you continue to make the same mistakes over and over, just like your friend Joan. If you choose the second option, on the other hand, you open yourself up to learning. And in the process of learning the lesson God has for you, you will build a far stronger relationship than you've ever been in before."

Elizabeth nodded. "So we just need to get to work and learn the lesson God has placed in front of us, whatever that is."

Dr. Scott looked pleased. "I couldn't have said it better myself. You have a great way with words."

Elizabeth accepted the compliment gracefully. "Thanks. That brings me to my second question. What if I'm too tired to start working on the relationship right now? What if I'm sick of all of the fighting and just want to coast for a while?"

Dr. Scott hesitated just a moment, then said, "I understand perfectly. And the answer to the question is, 'Because that's not one of your choices.' Do you understand?"

Elizabeth looked upset. "No, and I think I might be offended. You don't get to decide for me what my choices are."

Dr. Scott smiled. "Please don't be offended. It has nothing to do with me. I have come to understand that relationships are always doing one of two things–in any significant relationship, at any given time, we are either growing closer and closer together or we are drifting further and further apart. Like a plant, we are always either growing or dying. In the world that our transformational God has created, one of those two things is always happening. So coasting or staying the same is simply not one of our options."

Elizabeth looked a bit confused. "So you're saying that I can't coast because in reality that choice doesn't exist."

"Right," confirmed Dr. Scott. "And since the only two choices are those I've described, anyone who says 'I'm just coasting right now' is, in reality, allowing the relationship to get worse and worse. Is that really what you want?"

Elizabeth thought for a moment and then said, "No, because it would mean that later on it would take even more work to fix it than it would take right now."

Dr. Scott nodded vigorously. "Exactly! And I can promise you that at that later time you will be even more tired than you are now."

Elizabeth clearly understood. "So even though I am indeed weary from playing TAG, as you would say, this is the best shot that I will ever get at making my marriage right."

"Yes. If you sincerely want to have a good relationship, you need to start now. In God's world, there is only one time—right now."

"That's helpful," Elizabeth replied. "It's hard to hear, but it's helpful. I'm starting to understand now why Karen is always saying, 'A difficult truth is better than an easy lie.' I bet she got that from you."

Dr. Scott turned serious for a moment. "It's true that I care so much about my clients that I'll tell them the truth, even if it's not what they think they want to hear. So, what's your third concern?"

Now Elizabeth became extremely hesitant. "I'm not sure I even love Joe anymore. Why would I work hard for eight or ten weeks on this marriage when I am not even sure that Joe is the right one for me? I agree with you that drifting along is not the answer, but why not just end it with Joe and find someone that's more suited to me?"

Dr. Scott jumped right in. "Thanks for being so honest. Here's the deal. If I told you that I was in a terrible marriage, that it was all the fault of my wife, Rose, and that I was going to divorce her so I could go and find the right person for me, do you know what would happen?"

"No," responded Elizabeth, looking confused.

"Within two years I would be married to her sister."

"Why do you say that?" asked Elizabeth.

Dr. Scott replied, "Because I would not have learned anything or changed in any way, which means that I would still be exactly the same person and therefore would continue to pick exactly the same sort of person to date and to marry."

Elizabeth responded thoughtfully, "So you're saying that if I left the relationship now, without learning the things God wants to teach me, I would soon be in the same place I am now."

"Right," confirmed Dr. Scott. "Except that in the meantime you would have wrecked your immediate family, alienated yourself from Joe's side of the extended family, cut your kid time in half, created a financial hardship for yourself and everyone else, and virtually forced your friends to pick sides."

Elizabeth flinched. "That's harsh."

Dr. Scott shook his head. "No–just factual. If you don't work on the issues you need to work on, whatever they are, then you will continue to make the same mistakes everywhere you go. As Rose is always saying, 'Everywhere I go, there I am.' For my life to change, I have to change me first. That's why Jesus challenged us in Matthew 7 to quit focusing on the speck in our brother's eye and to focus instead on the log in our own eye."

Elizabeth nodded in understanding.

Dr. Scott continued. "So if you blame all of your problems on Joe and leave him, instead of working on the log in your own eye, you will continue to have all of the same problems you have now, PLUS your family will no longer attend church together, celebrate birthdays together, go on family vacations together, eat together, or do any of the things that families do together. And for what?"

Elizabeth responded, "I get it. I would STILL have to learn whatever lesson it is that God is trying to teach me. And meanwhile, nothing and no one in my family would ever be the same."

"Exactly. I see SO many people who blame their partners for their problems and hastily leave their marriages, only to come to the horrible realization later that it was all a terrible, terrible mistake."

Elizabeth grimaced. "That would be an awful feeling."

"Honestly, it's tragic," agreed Dr. Scott.

"Okay, I'll give it my best shot," Elizabeth promised. "I'll work hard on the log in my own eye."

Dr. Scott said, "Good for you. Here's how I always think about it. No matter what, I'm going to need to work out my issues with somebody. Wouldn't it be better if that somebody was my lifetime partner, the one God had picked especially for me, the one I shared a history with, the one I had build a life with, the parent of my children, the one who has become a part of my extended family, the one who lives with me, and the only one who will ever care as intensely about my children as I do?"

Elizabeth perked up. "Wow, when you say it like that, it really makes sense."

"Thanks. For me, the question is never 'Why would I work so hard on the relationship I already have?' The question, given everything that is at stake, is 'Why on earth would I not?'"

"Good point," said Elizabeth. "I am going to quit asking myself why I would work on this marriage and start reminding myself of all of the reasons why I truly want this marriage to be good. And I am going to keep asking God what He wants me to learn, instead of blaming everything on Joe."

Dr. Scott cautioned her. "There are no guarantees. But you owe it to yourself and to everyone in your family to work on the things you need to work on and to find out if the marriage could then work in the glorious way that you and God would want it to work."

Joe nodded his head passionately. "I'm with you and Elizabeth on that one, doctor. After all, what do we have to lose by trying? What are eight or ten weeks of effort, compared to a lifetime of regrets? I promised God that I would honor Elizabeth in all that I did and this feels like a very honoring thing to do."

Dr. Scott looked pleased. "I'm glad you both agree. It's important that you both be committed to the process. God gave us free will, which means He will only help and guide us through the process after we make a clear decision that we are open to that help and guidance."

"Can we start the process today?" asked Elizabeth eagerly. "Now that we both have decided to change, I want to do something right now that will start to make things better."

Smiling, Dr. Scott said, "Actually, the two of you have started making things better already. When you made the mutual decision to change, it put you on the same team, as opposed to being on competing teams, the way you were when you came in. I'm guessing that this is already as connected as the two of you have felt for some time. Is that true?"

Joe grinned sheepishly and said, "Doctor, you know us too well already."

Dr. Scott shook his head. "No, I'm just trying to help you to understand a really important truth."

"What's that?" Joe wondered.

"It's this: the instant you both decide that you want things to be different, they ARE different. That's how fast God works."

"Wow, that's a powerful thought," Joe said excitedly.

Dr. Scott nodded. "Yes, it is. And in this case it means that the instant the two of you decided you wanted a better marriage, you had one."

Elizabeth clapped her hands in joy and exclaimed, "This is as hopeful as I have felt in a very long time."

Dr. Scott smiled at her. "Good. We're going to build upon that hope in just a minute. But first I want you both to do something for me."

"What's that?" Joe asked.

Dr. Scott responded, "I would like for you both to look at me carefully and notice what you see."

"Okay," said Joe, "although I have to tell you, it feels weird."

"Yes, I believe it does. Thanks for going along with my request. Now without moving your head or your eyes, please put your right hand immediately in front of your face–so close that it's almost touching your nose."

After Joe and Elizabeth had complied with his odd request, Dr. Scott asked, "What do you notice about me now?"

Puzzled, Elizabeth responded, "I can hardly see you at all."

"Exactly," said Dr. Scott. "Even though I haven't changed or moved in any way, your ability to see me clearly has been almost completely eliminated."

"What's your point?" Elizabeth wondered, in a tone that was a bit challenging.

Dr. Scott noted the tone but simply continued on. "The hand that blocks your view of me is just like the resentments that each of you has been carrying around. Those resentments have kept you from seeing the other person clearly. Now instead of seeing them through God's eyes, all you can see are your resentments. So you tell yourself that the other person has changed for the worse. But that's a lie. They haven't moved or changed in any way. The only thing that has changed is your ability to see them clearly."

Elizabeth asked in wonder, "So everything that once was good about Joe, everything that attracted me to him in the first place, is still true?"

"Yes," confirmed Dr. Scott. "In fact, he has probably gotten better at all of those things over time. Everything that used to be good about him is now great."

Elizabeth was quiet for a long time. "I never thought about that until now, but it's absolutely true. Joe used to really care about people but he never knew how to show it. Now he is far more comfortable giving praise and showing affection to people and they can really tell that he cares. In fact, they kind of perk up whenever he's around."

Joe could hardly sit still. "Doctor, you're incredible. What you're saying is SO true. Elizabeth has always been good at explaining things, but now she is absolutely amazing. She can take even the most complex ideas and lay them out in ways that people can understand immediately. It's really something to see."

Dr. Scott responded, "I'm pleased that the two of you are so willing to drop your resentful blinders and to see the other person for who they really are–the great and wonderful child of God they've always been and the even greater person they are becoming. That will make your homework assignment go even more smoothly."

"We have to do homework, like we're back in school?" Joe asked, teasing Dr. Scott.

"Yes, I'm afraid so," replied Dr. Scott, smiling. "In fact, the homework is the most important part of the entire process."

Joe made a big show of relenting. "Okay, okay, what do we have to do?"

"You need to get back to seeing each other through God's eyes. As a first step in that direction, you will each need to make a list of everything about the other person that is precious to you."

Joe hesitated and then asked, "That's it?"

Dr. Scott continued, "Then you need to sit by each other, turn toward each other, hold hands, and take turns reading your lists to each other."

"That's going to feel sort of artificial," Joe protested.

Dr. Scott nodded his agreement. "Everything does until it becomes part of our routine. That's why you are going to do this every day."

"Every day!?" Joe exclaimed.

Dr. Scott smiled, as if at a beloved child. "Don't act like this is some sort of punishment. Trust me—after you've done it a few times, it will become the favorite part of your day–the part you look forward to all day."

Joe looked thoughtful for a moment and then said, "Doctor, you obviously know what you are doing, so I am going to choose to believe you. Even if it does feel artificial at first, I'll keep practicing, believing that pretty soon it will start to feel more natural."

"I appreciate your willingness to persevere. Elizabeth, are you also willing to keep practicing the homework I've assigned until it feels more natural?"

Elizabeth shifted uncomfortably in her chair. "Dr. Scott, my concern is not that the process will feel artificial or mechanical. My concern is that it will feel very uncomfortable."

Dr. Scott smiled. "Well, if it does, that should be a good sign to you."

"What?" asked Elizabeth, looking a bit upset.

"The behaviors that feel comfortable to us are the ones we have been doing all along. Have those old behaviors been helpful to you?"

Elizabeth looked even more upset. "No, that's why we're here."

Dr. Scott nodded. "Precisely. If you felt uncomfortable, that would mean you were no longer doing things the old way. That would be a good sign, wouldn't it—a sign that you were choosing transformation?"

Elizabeth burst out laughing. "So if I'm uncomfortable that means I'm doing it right?"

"See how smart you are?"

Blushing, Elizabeth acknowledged Dr. Scott's compliment with a smile.

Dr. Scott concluded, "God is always calling us to step outside of our joyless comfort zone, where He can't use us, into our joyful new life, where everything we do builds the Kingdom. The goal is NOT to remain as you were—permanently comfortable, unhappy, and ineffective. The goal is to be filled with joy and to become powerfully effective, which requires that you first be temporarily uncomfortable."

Elizabeth grinned. "Okay, you win. I'll choose to be temporarily uncomfortable, in order that I might become incredibly happy and useful."

"Good for you."

Joe raised his hand. "Doctor Scott, I have one last question before we go. How does this homework assignment relate to the game of TAG that you were explaining to us?"

Dr. Scott was chagrined. "Gosh, I almost forgot to talk about that. Thank you for reminding me."

Joe smiled and said, "Glad to help–keeping things on track is sort of my specialty."

Dr. Scott smiled back and said, "Great–that specialty will come in handy, I'm sure. There are actually two reasons why I'm assigning you this homework. The first relates to what I call The 90/10 Rule."

Joe responded, "The 90/10 Rule?"

"Yes. All of us do things right about 90% of the time and make mistakes about 10% of the time. When we play TAG, we're always looking for a way to make the other person IT, which means we are always watching for the 10%."

Joe nodded, sadly. "So we ignore the 90% and pounce on the 10%."

"Right. In healthy relationships, on the other hand, we do exactly the opposite. We do what Paul suggests in Philippians 4—we focus on everything that is good and right and wonderful about the other person."

"Sounds like falling in love," Joe said with a smile.

Dr. Scott agreed, passionately. "It is exactly like that. Now, I know that a lot of people say falling in love is an illusion and that the illusion always fades over time."

"My girlfriends were saying that just the other day!" exclaimed Elizabeth.

Dr. Scott responded, "Yes, it's a popular notion but it's actually a lie."

"Really? Falling in love is not an illusion?" Elizabeth appeared doubtful.

Dr. Scott shook his head. "Nope. Being in love is actually the closest we can ever come to seeing the absolute truth about the other person. It's like we see them exactly as God sees them."

Elizabeth looked doubtful. "Being in love is actually seeing the truth about the other person?"

"Sure. Remember that hand exercise we just did?"

She nodded her head. "Yes."

Dr. Scott asked, "Was your view of me the most accurate when you had your hand in front of your face or when you did not?"

"When I didn't, obviously," said Elizabeth, with a trace of impatience.

Again Dr. Scott simply continued. "Right. And that's how it is when we are in love. We have no resentments, no filters that get in the way, no biases, and so we are free to see everything that is great about the other person."

Elizabeth shook her head in wonderment. "Wow, this blows my mind. So being in love is actually the truth."

"Yes, because when we are in love, we see the 90% clearly."

"What about the 10%?" Elizabeth asked.

Dr. Scott responded, "Good question. When we are in love, we recognize that the 10% is not who they really are–it's just the part of themselves they are still working on. So we see it but we don't worry about it or judge it, because we know they'll get better at it. This leaves us free to celebrate everything that is already wonderful about them."

Elizabeth brightened considerably. "It is so liberating to think of it like that."

Dr. Scott nodded. "And here's the best part. In the process of our celebrating everything that is great about them, they grow into their best self. That's why God is always wanting us to know how precious we are—when we recognize the truth about ourselves, we start to become that precious person."

"So it's like a self-fulfilling prophecy," said Elizabeth, clearly understanding the concept.

"Exactly," said Dr. Scott excitedly, "and it works in both directions."

"What do you mean?" she wondered.

"Over these past few months, how did you think of Joe?"

Elizabeth grimaced. "I had a very negative picture of him in my mind."

"Right. And what happened to his behavior?" Dr. Scott asked.

Elizabeth opened her eyes wide. "It got worse and worse."

Dr. Scott nodded. "In other words, when you focused on the 10%, he became less and less his true self."

Elizabeth shivered. "That's almost spooky."

"Yes, it can be almost frightening to realize the extent to which we actually create the world around us by the way that we think."

Elizabeth beamed. "I get it. By being in love with Joe, I am seeing what is actually true about him–I am seeing the man that he really is. And in seeing that, I am actually doing God's work—I am helping Joe to become a more and more perfect expression of the man God created him to be."

"Bingo."

"Wow. I'm blown away," replied Elizabeth, clearly impressed.

"Joe, does what we've been talking about make sense to you?"

"Yes, and I am really excited to think that being in love is the truth. Elizabeth is right–that is a really, really liberating thought."

Dr. Scott looked pleased. "I'm glad to hear you say that. The two of you have been living in a prison and liberation is indeed God's goal for you."

Joe smiled at that thought and then said, "There's one thing I'm still curious about. You said there were two reasons why the 'What's Precious About You' list would help us to quit playing TAG. The first reason was because the list would help us to start focusing on the 90%, instead of the 10%. What was the second reason?"

Dr. Scott turned toward him and said, "Thanks for reminding me. See, I knew your ability to stay on track would be helpful to us."

Joe simply waited expectantly.

Dr. Scott explained. "The second reason is this. In TAG, no one ever gives anyone else a compliment."

Joe wrinkled his brow. "Why not?"

"Think about it. If you and I are playing TAG, one of us HAS to be IT–that's the rule. And so, if I give you a compliment, praise your efforts, or lift you up in any way, what would that mean about me?"

"That would mean that you had to be IT," said Joe, proud of his insight.

"Right. It would mean that I was volunteering to be IT. No one would EVER do that–that's a suicide mission!" joked Dr. Scott.

Joe laughed.

Dr. Scott continued, "So by writing your lists and then sharing them with each other every day, you will be breaking the game of TAG in two explicit ways: you will be consciously choosing to focus on the 90%, rather than on the 10%, and you will be giving the kinds of compliments that are totally absent in the game.

Now here is what's really great. In the process, you will be radically changing the way that you think about the other person."

"Why is that so important?" Joe asked.

"Because everything in life always goes in this order: Think, Feel, Do."

Joe shook his head and said, "I'm not tracking with you."

"Yes, sometimes I'm too cryptic," Dr. Scott acknowledged. "What I meant to say was that our thinking totally drives our emotions and our emotions totally drive our behavior.

Here's why that is so important in this case. Doing the precious list every day will help you to see the other person more accurately—to think differently about them. This simple act of getting your thinking straight will have the added benefit of changing your feelings immediately. You will notice that you are starting to fall back in love with Elizabeth. And feeling in love, of course, will have a major impact on the way you treat her. Thus, in this one simple exercise, you will begin to change your thinking, your feeling, and your doing."

Joe nodded thoughtfully. "I think I understand, but that's a lot to absorb all at once. It may take me a while to truly grasp the significance of what you just said."

Dr. Scott nodded sympathetically. "Honestly, you don't have to understand it all yet. If you just do what I have asked you to do, you will see the process I've described unfolding right in front of you. And you will begin to understand why Jesus was constantly challenging people to think differently. All godly transformation requires a radical change in our thinking."

"Dr. Scott, at first I thought you were exaggerating when you said that we would be able to see an improvement in our marriage within a week. But now I can see it's true. If we spend the next week doing what you've asked, we will feel better, for sure."

Dr. Scott smiled and said, "I'm glad to hear you can tell that that's true. Would you be willing to make one small change in your thinking right now?"

"Sure, of course," Joe replied willingly.

"Good. When you say, 'If we spend the next week doing what you've asked,' you plant a small seed of doubt in your own mind. Your thinking is not completely clear and that lack of clarity will interfere with your attempts to change your feeling and your doing."

"That's fascinating," Joe responded. "And I can tell that you're right. How is this? 'When we spend the next week doing as you've asked, we will get better, for sure.'"

"That's a much more powerful statement," Dr. Scott pointed out, "and it leaves you with a far clearer picture of your success. That clear picture is critically important, because all transformational thinking begins with a clear vision.

Joe nodded his assent. "Yes, saying it that way both clarifies my vision and solidifies my thinking."

Dr. Scott turned toward Elizabeth. "Are you ready to make the same commitment?"

She grinned. "I'm not only ready, I'm totally pumped. I can't wait to get started."

"That's literally true," responded Dr. Scott.

"Pardon?" asked Elizabeth.

"You can't wait to get started. If you put your assignment off for even one day, you won't do it," Dr. Scott explained.

Elizabeth pretended to cross her heart and said, "I'll make my list tonight, as soon as the kids are in bed, and I'll share the list with Joe as soon as I'm finished."

Dr. Scott nodded, turned back toward Joe and asked, "Joe, are you ready to make the same promise?"

"Absolutely!"

"Great," replied Dr. Scott. "In the meantime, let's set up a time for the two of you to come back next week, when I'll teach you the next steps in the process. I can promise you that from here on out your journey will get even more interesting and exciting."

SUMMARY OF CHAPTER 2

- It is incredibly important to be in right relationship, vertically and horizontally. In fact, our entire faith is about creating, building, and expanding powerful relationships, with God and with one another.
- If we are in wrong relationship it is because we are playing TAG, a game in which doing what is right takes a back seat to avoiding being wrong.
- Rule #1 in any abusive or addictive family (and in the game of TAG) is this:

  If I can prove that you're wrong, I can be as mean to you as I want and it's your fault.

- The three corollaries of Rule #1 are:

  There are no loving or intimate conversations. Instead, every interaction quickly degenerates into an argument.

  Every one of those arguments is really just the same argument over and over.

  That repeated argument is an argument about who is NOT WRONG (because in the game of TAG, to be wrong is to invite abuse. That's Rule #1!!).

- The only three ways of interacting are: factual, intimate, and TAG.
- This means that all of us play TAG at least some of the time.
- It's never too late to transform your relationships. You can start today. In fact, you must.
- Relationships are always becoming closer and closer (more and more intimate) or drifting further and further apart (TAG). Thus, "coasting" or

staying the same, no matter how tempting an option it may seem, is not one of your choices. A plant is always either growing or dying.

- If you don't choose to change in the context of <u>this</u> relationship, you will just create a similar relationship with your <u>next</u> partner, while wreaking havoc in the process.
- You change by looking at the log in your own eye, not by seeing the speck in your partner's eye. If you want God to transform your relationship, you must be willing to let Him start with you.
- As soon as you choose to be different, you are different; all change starts with a decision.
- Your first decision must be to see your partner through God's eyes—you must decide to see them as they truly are.
- Everything that was once great about your partner still is great. The 90-10 Rule still applies, and you will realize this the instant you choose to see beyond your resentments.
- You saw your partner clearly when you fell in love and your clarity of vision helped them to become the person you believed them to be. That same self-fulfilling prophecy has probably been happening a lot lately, except in reverse.
- Everything in your life follows this order: Think-Feel-Do.
- Thus, your thinking must become clear, if you wish to change the way you feel about your partner and the way you behave toward them.
- That is also why the "precious list" is so important–it is the first step in the process of consciously changing the way that you think.
- This decision to think differently about your partner will immediately begin to generate a new set of emotions and a new range of behaviors. In other words, it will create the possibility of intimacy.
- If you are serious about your faith, you must start now.

EXERCISE #1

These exercises are an opportunity for you to learn right along with Joe and Elizabeth. Dr. Scott is right–most of the important results of the work done during therapy take place when you do the homework. So, I strongly suggest that you do this exercise, together with all of the upcoming exercises, in order that you might gain the maximum benefit from the workbook.

The Precious List can contain traits you admire (like a good sense of humor), specific recent behaviors that were precious to you (like a specific funny comment they made), skills they possess (like being a good cook or a great parent), physical attributes you love (like their goofy smile or their sexy appearance), or anything else you see as being precious (like the way they treat others or the depth of their faith).

Remember to keep adding to the list as you go–the better the relationship gets, the more you will recognize all that is precious about them. And, of course, the reverse is also true—the more you recognize what is precious about them, the better the relationship will get!

What's Precious To Me About ______________________________ Is:

CHAPTER 3:

Seeing the Game Differently: The 50-50 Rule

"Welcome back. How did the homework go?"

Joe was smiling. "Dr. Scott, I'm pleased to report that for the first time in a long time I'm actually happy."

Dr. Scott returned the smile. "Really? What happened?"

"We did our 'you're precious to me' assignment that first night, just like we promised we would, and it went great."

"What happened?"

Elizabeth jumped in. "When we sat by each other, held hands, and told each other what was precious about each other, it was almost like our first date."

"What do you mean?" Dr. Scott inquired.

Elizabeth replied slowly, "I felt shy, like I was on our first date. But I also could tell that I did still have a lot of positive feelings for Joe, just like I did at first. It was just as you told us, when I took the hand down from in front of my face, there he was–the man I fell in love with. I consciously decided to see him through God's eyes, just like you asked us to, and in the instant I chose to see him that way, it was true. You were right!"

"I'm so glad. Sounds like the two of you are off to a great start."

Joe nodded in agreement and added, "The exercise helped us both to remember why we had gotten into this relationship in the first place. It seems weird to say this now, but I honestly had forgotten how fun it is just to be with Elizabeth and how much I enjoy just being in her presence."

Dr. Scott replied, "I understand. When a couple plays TAG to the point that the game starts to take over the relationship, there is such a strong emphasis on 'what's wrong with you'—on the 10%—everything good just gets lost in the shuffle."

Joe clearly understood and said, "Yeah, it's crazy. And it made us so unhappy."

Dr. Scott summarized by saying, "So now the difference is clear to you both. When you look at each other through the world's eyes, you will focus on the negative and you will feel terribly unhappy. When you look at each other through God's eyes, you will focus on all that is precious and you will be filled with joy. A pretty simple choice, wouldn't you say?"

Elizabeth nodded and said, "Yes, now that we understand the two options. It is a simple choice, indeed."

Dr. Scott continued, "In God's world, it is never 'A or B.' It is always 'A and B,' especially with respect to healing. And here is a perfect example. To your mutual credit, you both did indeed choose to see the other person differently. And in the process, I am guessing you each had the chance to see yourself differently too."

"What do you mean?" asked Elizabeth.

Dr. Scott responded, "Well, if I interact negatively with my wife, Rose, it does indeed make <u>her</u> feel bad about herself. That part is obvious,

I suppose. What perhaps is not so obvious is that it also makes me feel terrible about myself."

"In what way?" Elizabeth wondered.

"It makes it hard for me to feel proud of myself," Dr. Scott pointed out. "How good can I feel about being the guy who harshly criticizes his own sweet wife and the mother of his children–the one woman in the world he has sworn to honor and protect?"

Elizabeth nodded. "That's a good point. I hadn't thought about it like that."

Dr. Scott continued. "On the other hand, when I treat my honey lovingly and I can tell that my caring for her is helping her to feel special, giving her hope. . . well, that makes me feel pretty darn good about myself–it fills me with a powerful sense of purpose. I have always felt that the fastest way for a person to enhance their own self-esteem is to actively build up and care for those around them."

"I see what you mean. That's helpful." replied Elizabeth.

Joe interjected, "Then my constantly critical dad must have felt terrible about himself all of the time."

Dr. Scott nodded his head sadly. "Yes, that's where TAG became one of those awful types of self-fulfilling prophecies."

"In what way?" Joe wondered.

"Your father treated you poorly, which left him feeling ashamed of himself. What is the one thing a person wants to do when they feel like they're the bad one?"

Joe responded immediately, "They want to tag someone else–to make someone else IT, instead of themselves."

"Exactly. His harsh treatment of you made him feel like he was IT, which made him want to tag you, which led to harsh treatment, which made him feel even worse about himself. And so the cycle continued."

Joe shrugged and said, "Sounds kind of hopeless, like a constant downward spiral."

Dr. Scott agreed. "As long as TAG continues, it IS hopeless and it IS a downward spiral. Remember how I told you that relationships were always either getting better and better or worse and worse–that those were the only two options?"

"Yes," Joe said, in a matter-of-fact tone.

"Well, that would be an example of worse and worse."

Joe looked bleak. "I get it."

Dr. Scott brightened. "That's probably enough of the gloom and doom of the past. Let's get back to the present; tell me more about how the homework went."

Elizabeth started by saying, "There were only two hard parts. The first was that we got out of the habit when Joe was gone overnight on a business trip, and the second was that by the end of the week I was bored reading Joe the same list."

"Let's take those problems one at a time. First, you need to make sure that you have a Plan B," stated Dr. Scott.

Elizabeth looked puzzled. "What's a Plan B?"

"Anytime one of you is going to be gone or unavailable at your usual time, you need to decide ahead of time when you will talk–you need to make a clear Plan B."

"So when Joe is going to be gone or I am going to be at a meeting until late. . ."

"When Joe is going to be gone, you need to have a time picked out when you will share your lists with each other over the phone. It's not as good as doing it in person but it is far better than not doing it at all."

She smiled, saying, "That does seem good. That way, I would still get to hear good things about myself every day. Plus, we would stay in the habit of reviewing our lists each day."

Dr. Scott nodded in affirmation. "Exactly. And if you are going to be out in the evening, then the two of you need to decide ahead of time that you're going to share your lists with each other before you go, or after you come home, or over the phone during the day, or whatever else works for you. Anything is fine, as long as you are both clear on the plan."

"Great–I understand about Plan B. What do we do about getting bored with the list?"

"Just remember that the list is a work in progress," Dr. Scott explained. "You both are free to add things every day, as you think of them. That way, the listener will get to hear new great things about themselves every day, the speaker will have more fun, and you both will stay focused on the 90%."

"So it's good to keep adding to the list."

"Absolutely. It's also fine to vary the presentation," Dr. Scott added.

"What do you mean?" Elizabeth wondered.

Dr. Scott elaborated. "You don't always have to just read the list. On some days you might want to name just one thing that makes Joe precious to you and then give him lots of specific examples, so that he can really see what you mean. On other days you might want to be giving him a hand massage or a back massage or a foot massage while you read your list. You might write him a love letter that day instead of reading the list, or have the kids add their own items to the list and read their part of the list to their dad."

Elizabeth responded excitedly, "Those ideas all sound fun to me. I'm going to start getting a little more creative with what we are calling our 'precious time.'"

"I'm glad for you. I hope you have fun with it. Just make sure you keep using the list in some way each day and you'll be fine," replied Dr. Scott.

"I promise I will. In fact, I look forward to it."

Dr. Scott turned to Joe and asked, "Do you have any other questions about sharing your lists with each other?"

Joe shook his head. "No, but I am very curious about what comes next. I remember you saying that the process would keep getting more and more interesting and I am very much looking forward to that."

Dr. Scott smiled in anticipation. "It really is true–the more you learn about dropping TAG and creating a whole new marriage, the more interesting it gets. I'm glad you're ready."

"I am ready," affirmed Joe. "So, what's next?"

"Next we get to talk about teamwork and about what I call 'The 50-50 Rule.'"

Joe smiled. "Okay, I'll bite. What on earth is 'The 50-50 Rule' and why is that the next thing that we need to learn?"

Dr. Scott began by saying, "The entire game of TAG is based on the assumption that whenever there is a problem, somebody has to be IT. In other words, there has to be one person who is totally to blame for the entire problem. There has to be a bad one. "

"Right. And so . . ." Joe waited expectantly.

Dr. Scott continued, saying, "Now that you are beginning to remember your beloved partner is extremely precious to you, you realize that she can't possibly be the bad one and that you can never again justify treating her harshly or making her IT."

Joe looked anxious and asked, "So what's the alternative–do I always have to be IT, instead?"

Dr. Scott looked at Joe gently and responded, "No, we are not going to recreate your family of origin."

"Thank goodness."

"I would ask that you notice, however, how fast you were to jump to that conclusion–to fall right back into that old role of being permanently

IT. You will need to be mindful of that as we continue," Dr. Scott pointed out.

"What exactly do you mean by that?" Joe wondered.

"Thank you for asking," Dr. Scott paused, then continued on. "What I mean is that I would like for you to actively pay attention–to notice all of the times when you immediately assume that you're IT."

"I'm willing," replied Joe. "But how can I tell when I'm making that assumption?"

Dr. Scott explained, "As soon as you feel upset, get sick to your stomach, and see yourself either withdrawing or getting defensive–'explaining' things–you can be sure that you believe yourself to be IT."

Joe nodded. "That makes sense. What do I need to do differently when I notice myself acting that way?"

"First," answered Dr. Scott, "don't judge or condemn yourself for having made that mistake. That's not helpful. In fact, it actually keeps the pattern going."

"In what way?"

Dr. Scott responded, "Well, if I'm judging myself, I'm saying that I'm bad–I'm making myself IT, am I not?"

Joe laughed. "If I get down on myself for being IT, I just make myself even more IT!"

"Right–hardly the way to break that cycle."

Joe, still laughing, asked, "So, what can I do instead?"

Dr. Scott thought for a moment and then said, "Just notice it, smile to yourself, and think 'Gosh, I set a new record that time–only two-tenths of a second from Elizabeth's innocent question to my being IT. I'm getting really fast at this!' or something like that."

Joe smiled and said, "I can do that. It'll be a good way for me to use my twisted sense of humor."

Dr. Scott returned the smile and said, "Great. Anything that breaks the cycle we get into ('Oh no, I'm going to be IT'; 'Oh no, I'm going to be IT'; 'Oh no, I'm going to be IT') helps us come back to reality, which allows us to begin making a conscious choice as to how we want to proceed."

Joe suddenly looked confused. "But once I realize I can make a different choice, what choice do I have? If Elizabeth isn't IT, don't I have to be IT?"

Shaking his head rapidly, Dr. Scott responded, "In the game of TAG, that IS the only other alternative. But once we start seeing all that is precious about each and every one of God's children, we realize that we can't be IT either. After all, we're precious too–that's why our partner keeps reading us their precious list."

Joe persisted. "So what happens when two of God's precious children have a problem?"

Dr. Scott put his index finger to his lips, pondered the question, then started by saying, "Let me ask you both this question. When you were a kid, running around outside playing the childhood version of Tag, who was on your team?"

Joe and Elizabeth were silent for a moment, looking at each other. Finally, she spoke up and said, "I don't get it. There was no one on your team. It was every person for themselves."

Dr. Scott agreed. "Exactly. It's the same way in TAG. There is no one on your team. Even in a marriage, everyone feels and acts as if they are totally alone."

After a long, silent pause, Elizabeth began to cry softly. "It's true. By the time we came to see you I had begun to act as if I truly was alone. I was making almost all of my decisions without consulting Joe and I didn't seek to include him in any of my activities. It was like I had dropped the word "we" right out of my vocabulary. And I was so lonely."

Joe looked sad too. "We let each other down. We were only looking out for ourselves, instead of looking out for each other."

Dr. Scott nodded. "Right. In TAG there is no team. It's always 'me against you' whenever there is a problem. The only way for me not to be the bad one is for you to be the bad one."

Joe shook his head. "That's an ugly game."

Dr. Scott agreed. "Yes, Joe, it is ugly in the way that every ungodly interaction is ugly. Fortunately, there is a whole different game to play–a God-led game that is a lot more fun and much more productive than making each other IT."

"What does that God-led game look like?" Joe asked hopefully.

"Instead of playing TAG, healthy families approach everything as a team. So when they have a conflict, Rule #1 in <u>their</u> game is: 'It's Never About You, It's Always About Us.' Or, as I call it, 'The 50-50 Rule.'"

Joe smiled. "I like the sound of this game already."

Dr. Scott responded, "That's good, because it's based on this fundamental truth–that every problem we have in a relationship can't possibly be either your fault or my fault, since it is always <u>our</u> fault."

"Always?" Joe asked skeptically.

"Yes, always," stated Dr. Scott emphatically. "<u>Every</u> struggle the two of you have is always exactly 50-50."

"I don't know about the 50-50 part," Elizabeth said slowly. "I think certain problems of ours are mostly my fault."

Dr. Scott shook his head and replied, "It's sweet of you to think so, but it's not helpful and it's not true. Without exception, you both contribute to every problem you have, to exactly the same degree."

Elizabeth was silent, pondering the doctor's words, when Joe burst out, "Doctor, if that was true, it would change everything."

"It is true and you're right–once you understand it, it does change everything."

"But Dr. Scott, how could it be true?" asked Elizabeth, still struggling with the concept.

"I understand why this is difficult for you to grasp. The two of you have played TAG for so long, starting way before you met each other, that it is hard for you to drop that distorted way of thinking. In fact, you have been thinking in those terms for so long that you have come to believe that your distorted way of thinking IS the truth. So when I finally tell you the real truth, you think that's the lie!"

Elizabeth persisted. "So what is the truth?"

Dr. Scott smiled and said, "The truth is that we marry people who have very similar strengths to ours and the flip side of our weaknesses."

Elizabeth shook her head and asked, "What does that mean, 'the flip side of our weaknesses'?"

Dr. Scott elaborated. "Let's say that there is a party for thirty single adults and that one of the attendees is a man who is a compulsive talker–he talks, talks, talks and he never listens. And let's say another person at the party is a woman similar in age who is a compulsive listener–she never talks at all, she just constantly smiles and nods her head."

"I'm with you," Elizabeth said, by way of encouragement.

Dr. Scott asked, "Now, what do you suppose are the odds that these two people will end up together before the night is over?"

Elizabeth shrugged and said, "Pretty good, I suppose."

"Actually," taught Dr. Scott, "there is a nearly 100% chance that they will end up together."

"Why do you say that?" Elizabeth asked, still clearly skeptical.

"Well, let's imagine how it will go. The compulsive talker guy will start talk, talk, talking to some woman. Pretty soon, she will be responding, by asking questions or offering insights, and the compulsive talker guy will think to himself, 'You're annoying. You don't listen.' And he will break off the conversation and start talk, talk, talking to some other woman. Within a moment or two, she also will be trying to get a word in edgewise, at which point he will think to himself, 'You don't get me.' And, in irritation, he again will break off the conversation and start talking with yet another woman."

Elizabeth nodded. "Now I get it. Until he bumps into the compulsive listener woman, all of his conversations will end in the same way."

Dr. Scott leaned forward in his chair and said enthusiastically, "Exactly! Then he bumps into her, as you said, and he thinks to himself, 'What a great woman. She listens so well! She really gets me.' And he continues talking to her. Before the night is over he will probably feel so comfortable with her that he will ask her out on a date."

"That poor woman," replied Elizabeth, with a grimace.

Dr. Scott smiled. "This is where you need to be careful, Elizabeth. That's your TAG thinking coming out–your thinking that there has to be one bad one."

"Are you saying he's not obnoxious?" she asked indignantly.

"No," Dr. Scott responded. "I'm just saying that this is a two-person game, as are all games."

Elizabeth looked puzzled. "So you're telling me that she plays a part in this game too?"

Dr. Scott elaborated by saying, "Of course. Let's look at the same party scenario from her perspective. She arrives at the party and right away some guy starts talking to her and she just smiles and nods her head. But pretty soon he's asking her questions–'What do you do for a living?' or 'Who else do you know at this party?' and she gets very uncomfortable and breaks off the conversation. A few minutes later, another guy starts talking to her and again she just smiles and nods. Pretty soon, though, he clearly is expecting a response. Again, she gets very uncomfortable and breaks off the conversation. This will continue to happen until, eventually, she encounters the compulsive talker guy. And she will stay in that conversation, just like the compulsive talker guy, because it will never make her uncomfortable."

Elizabeth tested her knowledge by responding, "And so the two of them may well go on to develop a relationship, in part because they have what you call the flip side of the same weakness."

"Right!" confirmed Dr. Scott. "See, these two people both have the same problem–neither one of them has a clue how to conduct themselves in a mutual, give-and-take conversation. He compensates for his lack of knowledge by talking all of the time, she compensates by listening all of the time, and they fit together like a hand and glove."

"Wow, so they would develop this odd relationship where he always talked and she always listened and it would be because <u>both</u> of them had a problem."

"Or, more precisely, because both of them had the flip side of the <u>same</u> problem," replied Dr. Scott, fine-tuning her thinking.

"Why would they settle for that kind of a relationship?" wondered Joe.

"That's a good question," responded Dr. Scott. "They settle for that form of relationship because it is a comfort zone for both of them. We humans have a huge preference for the status quo. We tend to keep doing what is familiar to us, even if it consistently leads to very negative consequences. It's like the Hebrew people did shortly after Moses led them out of their terrible slavery in Egypt, they began 'murmuring' that perhaps they should go back!"

Puzzled, Joe asked, "So that man and that woman would continue to interact in that odd, yet comfortable, way because that's the way they liked to interact?"

Dr. Scott shook his head. "Oh, no, they probably don't like it at all. Just because something is comfortable doesn't mean we like it. Did the Hebrew people like being slaves? No, our comfort zone is almost always diametrically opposed to what we would actually like to do or would want to do."

Joe looked skeptically at Dr. Scott and then asked, "Then why don't we do what we want to do instead?"

"In a word, fear."

"Fear?"

"Sure," responded Dr. Scott. "The fear of the unknown, the fear of making a mistake, the fear of looking foolish, the fear of what people will think, the fear of being wrong, and the fear of being known, to name a few. In other words, the fear of being IT."

Joe remained unconvinced. "That's it? Fear is all that keeps us from having what we want?"

"Yes," confirmed Dr. Scott, "but don't underestimate the importance of fear or its incredibly destructive power. There are many Christians who say that life in this world is a struggle between good and evil. That's close enough to the truth—I don't usually bother to correct them. But it's more perfectly understood as a struggle between love and fear."

Joe looked puzzled. "So if I choose love . . ."

"Then I choose to live in right relationship with God and with others. This requires that I step outside of my comfort zone, share God's love with all of the people in my life, live in community, and consistently choose transformation. In return I get to live a big life—a life filled with love, ministry, miracles, and unlimited possibilities."

"And if I choose fear?" Joe asked.

"Then I live in fearful isolation. I stay in my comfort zone, trapped in my very small life. Instead of choosing to be connected, I choose isolation. Instead of experiencing God's transformative power, I choose to be a powerless victim. And instead of choosing to create infinite possibilities, I choose boredom. My fear keeps me paralyzed. I feel stuck in my terrible unhappiness and I tell myself that I have no other options."

Joe opened his eyes wide. "Wow. Those are some powerful images."

Dr. Scott nodded his head in acknowledgment and waited.

"So I will immediately start moving toward the life that I want, as soon as I consciously decide to choose love instead of fear?"

"Precisely," confirmed Dr. Scott. "And isn't that exactly what has been happening right in front of your eyes? You used to be afraid to admit failure and you let that fear paralyze you into inaction. As a result, your marriage kept getting worse and worse.

Then you chose love—you set aside your fear, stepped outside of your comfort zone, decided that you wanted to be more connected to Elizabeth, and chose transformation. And immediately your marriage started to get better. In fact, it is getting better so quickly that in less than 60 days you will be well on your way to having exactly the marriage and the life you have always wanted."

"I'm impressed with myself," Joe said, laughing at his own joke.

"Way to not be IT!" responded Dr. Scott, teasing and being pleased for Joe at the same time.

Joe turned more serious for a moment. "So I decided not to let my fears stop me anymore and here I am, already changing."

"Right," replied Dr. Scott "Remember in our first meeting I said something to the effect that the very act of deciding to change changes us?"

"Yes," responded Joe. "I thought that was truly profound."

"Well, here's why that statement is true. The only thing that ever holds us back is our fear. As soon as we decide that we will no longer allow our fear to paralyze us, the growth process is free to begin. And it does begin immediately because that is what we were created to do."

"Always?" asked Joe doubtfully.

"Yes, always," replied Dr. Scott. "If you take a healthy seed, plant it into fertile ground, and give it water, will it immediately start growing?"

"Of course. That's what seeds do."

Dr. Scott nodded. "And we are just like that seed. We begin to grow immediately, as long as we are healthy seeds (are open to God's leading), who have been firmly planted (have made a clear decision to change), and are watered (are being taught the few simple techniques that I will teach you)."

Joe looked a bit uncertain. "That makes life seem so simple."

Dr. Scott agreed. "It is that simple. Everything in life that is true is simple."

Joe, by way of summary, said, "So as long as I stick to my decision, as long as I keep choosing love, I will be open to God's leading, I will continue to learn the concepts you are teaching us, and our marriage will continue to grow. The results will be almost automatic because we were literally created to be in right relationship with one another and with God."

"Yes," Dr. Scott cautioned, "but don't ever forget that those 'automatic' results are also miraculous."

"How can something that is automatic also be miraculous?"

Dr. Scott asked, "Is it a miracle when you plant a handful of seeds in good dirt and water them and that handful of tiny seeds eventually becomes an entire garden of vegetables?"

Joe gave his assent. "You're right; that is God's ultimate miracle–the miracle of life."

"As I said, everything that is true is also simple. And everything that is true and simple is also miraculous."

"I believe you, Dr. Scott. But I don't understand why you are making such a big point about the miraculous nature of the changes we are and will continue to be experiencing."

With great passion, Dr. Scott spoke, "Because you and Elizabeth will soon have a beautiful, God-led relationship. Once the two of you have established that sort of relationship, there will be only one thing that could destroy it. You will have only one enemy."

Joe was a bit taken aback. He asked, "And what will that be?"

Dr. Scott answered, "Complacency. The only way you could damage that new, beautiful connection that God is working powerfully to establish would be to take it for granted."

"What would happen then?" Joe asked.

"A few minutes ago I reminded you that relationships were always going in one of two directions."

"Right," Joe replied. "They are always either getting better and better or worse and worse."

"And so what do you suppose happens to your marriage the instant you fall away from your very clear decision to choose love?"

"It immediately starts to get worse and worse!" Joe exclaimed.

Dr. Scott nodded. "The techniques I am teaching you will always work–that part is almost automatic because God created us to be connected and is always leading willing hearts into deeper and deeper connections, with each other and with Him. But if you forget that this process is also a miracle, if you forget to be profoundly grateful every day, then you will start taking the relationship for granted—you will quit actively choosing love. At that point, your heart will no longer be open, you will quit learning, your miraculous new connection to each another will get weaker and weaker, and eventually you will end up back where you were before, except worse."

Joe got it. "So although I can be sure God will start to transform me the instant I ask Him, it is terribly important that I never take those transformational changes for granted."

Dr. Scott nodded. "Right. Good gardeners know that God will always work to miraculously multiply their efforts. However, they also know that the minute they get complacent–the instant that they choose to quit lovingly watering, weeding, and pruning—everything will come to a screeching halt, and very shortly that garden will be a mess again."

"The miracles may be almost automatic, but those miracles end the instant we take them for granted, because it is our gratitude for those miracles that helps us to remember to keep choosing love."

"Wow, Joe, I didn't know you were such a poet," teased Elizabeth.

Dr. Scott agreed. "That was beautifully said. And it makes it so clear why Paul said in I Thessalonians 5 that we were to give thanks in all circumstances. When we give thanks we are remembering the miraculous nature of the amazing gifts God has showered upon us. And when we see clearly the gifts which have come to us when we have chosen love, it helps us to remember that we must keep choosing love."

Joe replied, in a very serious tone, "I will dedicate my life to expecting miracles in my marriage and to thanking God every day for those miracles."

Dr. Scott patted him on the shoulder and said, "Good for you. I notice that we have drifted rather far afield, so let me summarize where we are.

1.) You now understand the importance of doing the 'why you are precious to me' lists each day and you will use Plan B meeting times and creative approaches to keep the process fresh and on track. This will help you to remember who the other person is and to break through TAG's lack of compliments and the game's destructive emphasis on the 10%.

2.) You also are beginning to understand that whereas in TAG everyone feels alone and blames each problem on a specific person, in reality we are never alone and every problem we experience is 50-50. Transformation begins the instant we realize that we are a team, that we each have the flip side of each other's weaknesses, and that we must work together to create a radically different sort of connection to each another.

3.) Thus, you can now see that your old question, 'Whose fault is this?' is actually a crazy question. A far better question would be, 'What are the unhelpful patterns we get into and what parts do each of us play in those patterns?' This immediately switches us from being enemies to being teammates–50-50 partners in everything, including the resolution of our problems.

4.) The only thing that keeps us stuck in our old patterns–our mutual comfort zones–is our fear. The instant we choose love, our fear (of being IT) no longer paralyzes us and we immediately begin to experience the miracle of transformation. We start to build the powerful relationships

God had in mind for us when He created us. And those relationships will continue to grow deeper every day, as long as we see them for the miracles that they are."

5.) The best way to remember that our new relationship is a miracle is to be grateful every day–to thank God for bringing our partner to us and to tell our partner every day how glad we are to have them in our lives. And that brings us right back to the precious lists!"

"That's a lot to learn in one day," commented Elizabeth.

Joe agreed and asked, "What is our next homework assignment, doctor?"

"I would ask that you do two things. First, continue sharing your 'precious lists' with each other every day as we've discussed, with two small twists."

Joe smiled. "That 'twists' thing makes me nervous."

Dr. Scott was reassuring. "No need to be nervous–it will be a sweet experience, actually."

"That sounds nice. What is it?" asked Elizabeth.

"Each night before you start reading your list, I would ask that you thank God for the precious person sitting next to you. And when you are done reading your lists, I would ask that you tell each another how grateful you are to have each other. This process will help each of you to feel even more precious and to keep choosing love."

Elizabeth smiled shyly. "That will be nice. Awkward, but nice."

"Joe, are you up for that?"

Joe grinned. "You know me, doc. I'll keep practicing until I get good at it."

Dr. Scott nodded in acknowledgment of the truth of that statement and then continued. "I'm proud of you both. The second thing I would ask that you do is to keep track of the unhelpful interactions you have–not in a blaming way, but in a scientific way."

Elizabeth asked, "Should we each carry a little notebook around with us?"

"Yes," Dr. Scott affirmed. "You should each do that because the sooner you record the incident the more accurately you will remember it and the more accurately you remember it the faster we can break the patterns."

"What should we be writing down?" she wondered.

"Everything you can remember about the interaction–the words that were said and unsaid, the feelings that triggered those words, the situations you were in. Everything."

Elizabeth looked uncertain and asked, "What will we do once we understand the patterns?"

Dr. Scott smiled gently and replied, "Don't get ahead of yourself. For right now, just notice the patterns and write down everything you notice. Is that okay?"

"I'll do that," she said agreeably. "This whole process is really just one big opportunity for me to learn to let go of control, isn't it?"

Laughing, Dr. Scott said, "See, you really are very smart! Joe, do you feel like you are also clear about the assignments?"

"Yes, Dr. Scott. We will continue to do our lists each day, with those 'twists' you added, and we will start to pay careful attention to our unhelpful patterns."

"I couldn't have summarized it better myself."

"Thanks," said Joe. "I'm more than willing to do the second half of our assignment, but I do have one concern."

"What's that?" asked Dr. Scott.

Joe paused and then responded, "I thought you said last week that the past didn't matter–that as soon as we learned some new ways to interact, we wouldn't even care what had happened in the past. I liked the sound of that because I hate the thought of dwelling on the past and on all of the mistakes we used to make. Do we really have to go back there?"

Dr. Scott listened carefully and then shook his head. "I'm not asking you to go back there at all. I'm asking you to notice problematic patterns that are occurring in the present."

"Why do we need to focus on our problems? Can't we just forget about them and move forward? I want to focus on solutions, not on problems," Joe insisted.

"Yes, that's what I want, too," agreed Dr. Scott.

"Then why the second part of our homework assignment?"

Dr. Scott paused, then said, "This will sound like I'm not answering your question, so hang with me for a moment."

"Okay."

Dr. Scott began, "I used to believe that the role of an expert was to come up with solutions. I now know differently."

Joe waited.

"I learned that I was wrong because I used to go to a mechanic who wasn't very good. I would begin to tell him what was wrong with my car and before I could finish he would say 'yeah, yeah' and he would go fix something–often the wrong thing, as it turned out. See, he thought the same thing I used to think–that it was the role of the expert to act like he knew the solution. As a result, he was incredibly unhelpful to me and my problems continued."

"Sounds like the place I go," reflected Elizabeth. "I don't like it there."

"Yeah," Dr. Scott said sympathetically, "that's a crummy experience. Now I take my car to a guy who really listens. He takes careful notes; then says to me, 'that tells me just where to look.' He hooks the car up to his computer, does a thorough analysis, comes back to me and says, 'Mister Scott, your third spark plug is broken.' At that point, even I know what to do."

"The point being?" asked Joe, with a trace of irritation.

Dr. Scott continued patiently. "The point being that the role of an expert is not to know the answers. The role of the expert is to help the other person to understand the problem so perfectly that the solution becomes self-evident."

Joe brightened noticeably. "As soon as we understand our unhelpful patterns, inside and out, it will be obvious to us what we need to do in order to change the old patterns."

"Precisely. We will focus on the problems only long enough to see the solution clearly. After that, every minute will be spent practicing and perfecting the solutions."

"That's fair," replied Joe. "I should have known that you would know what you were doing."

Dr. Scott chided him gently, saying, "Joe, you're not IT."

Joe looked startled. "What?"

Dr. Scott clarified his point by saying, "Asking a question or clarifying an assignment doesn't make you IT. Please don't do that to yourself."

Joe nodded sadly and said, "That's what you meant, isn't it?"

Dr. Scott looked lost. "Pardon?"

"That's what you meant before, when you said that I automatically assume that I am IT. I need to notice myself doing that, so that I can laugh at myself and break the cycle."

Dr. Scott nodded vigorously. "Right!"

"Oh, now I get it. And I'm with the program. I'll start writing down those unhelpful patterns, so that we can begin to understand them and begin to practice the self-evident solutions. And in the meantime, I won't make myself IT."

"Great," replied a smiling Dr. Scott. "I'll see the two of you next week."

SUMMARY OF CHAPTER 3

- When you set aside time each day to do the Precious List (with the "twists" that Dr. Scott added), you re-create your intimate connection and you also develop an important discipline–the discipline of spending time together each day. All great relationships are built upon this discipline.
- Focusing on their precious qualities helps to build your self-esteem. It's a true win-win. That's how it always is, in God's world.
- If you can't do the precious list at your usual time, make sure you have a Plan B.
- Be creative about the lists; add to them, focus on one trait, give massages, or have the kids join you in the process.
- Since the truth is that you are both precious, neither one of you can ever be IT. That's why in healthy families Rule #1 is: "It's Never About You, It's Always About Us." That's the 50-50 Rule, which puts an immediate end to TAG and to the painful loneliness it inevitably creates.
- The 50-50 Rule is always true because we choose as partners people who have similar strengths to ours and the exact flip side of our weaknesses.
- We cling to our weaknesses because of our fears.
- The instant we choose love, instead of being limited by those fears, transformation begins, naturally and miraculously.
- The way to make sure that these miracles continue to occur is to be grateful–to never take them for granted (because, remember, relationships never stay the same–we are always either growing closer and closer together or drifting further and further apart).
- The more perfectly we understand our destructive patterns, the more obvious the solution will become.

EXERCISE #2

Possible Examples

There are six ways in which you can (actively or passively) initiate or prolong a TAG-playing conversation.

1.) the statements that you make (or don't make)

Both the statements that you do make and the statements that you don't make can be a way to play TAG–a way to not be IT. Below are five common active TAG-playing statements, along with their passive parallels.

<u>**active form**</u> (the things you do say)

a.) "We wouldn't be having this problem if you hadn't…"

b.) "I would never have done it that way."

c.) "You always..." or "You never…"

d.) "You are going to make us late, again."

e.) "I can't trust you to…"

<u>**passive form**</u> (the things you don't say)

a.) You ignore the problem altogether, to your detriment and theirs.

b.) You think judgmental thoughts that you keep to yourself. When asked how you would have handled the situation, you pretend not to hear the question or to have no opinion.

c.) You never tell people what you want and then walk around feeling resentful that you never get what you want.

d.) You do not tell people that you are getting anxious until you are ready to explode and then you make too big a deal about something else.

e.) You do everything yourself and feel overwhelmed, just so you never have to sound needy or to trust anyone else.

Please note that both the active and passive responses lead to the same results. Problems go unresolved, constructive dialogue stops, needs go unmet, resentment builds, and teamwork ceases. In the end, the relationship is either damaged or destroyed.

2.) the questions that you ask (or don't ask)

active form

a.) "You payed how much for that?"

b.) "Didn't I already ask you to...?"

c.) "How could you have...?"

passive form

a.) You worry about the family's finances without ever telling your partner. Meanwhile, you go ever further into debt, while you ask yourself, "How much longer can we go on like this?"

b.) Instead of asking for help, you do the task yourself, in front of him, so that he will feel bad. When he asks you what's wrong, you say "nothing."

c.) Instead of honestly asking her about her thought process, you silently condemn her or ask others if they think she was wrong. (or at least agree that you were not wrong).

As you can see, each "question," whether asked or unasked, is just a way to be judgmental (to make others IT) while pretending to be doing something else–innocently asking for information or listening quietly, for example. The falseness of such a response will make others very uncomfortable, to the point where they will withdraw from the conversation. If this happens often enough in the same relationship, the two of you will start to experience one of those famous "communication problems."

And like most communication problems, this breakdown will occur not because the people lack the skills to communicate but because they lack the desire to do so. Most disconnections are the result of a fear-based decision, not a skill deficit.

3.) the unsolicited suggestions you provide

active form

a.) "Why don't you..."

b.) "If that happened to me I would..."

c.) "I think you need to..."

d.) "From now on, you should just..."

passive form

A judgmental look, a shake of the head when others are talking, a decision that is made (behind the scenes) "for their own good," a conversation about the person while they are absent (gossip), and the unwillingness to truly listen are all passive ways of giving unsolicited advice.

All of these active and passive ways of offering unsolicited advice send the message to the other person that he is incapable of running his own life. This undermining response will always leave him feeling judged and inferior–like he can not do anything right. After a while, he may quit trying altogether–a painful sort of self-fulfilling prophecy.

4.) the voice tones that you use (or don't use)

Much of what you do that is judgmental has more to do with the way you say things than with the things you actually say. Even the most innocent question ("How much did that cost?") becomes a judgment if you say it in a harsh tone, a louder than normal voice, or an argumentative manner.

Our rule of thumb is this–unless your tone, volume, and language clearly communicate the fact that the other person is precious to you, she will feel judged.

This rule of thumb applies to even the most mundane conversations and situations. You could say, "Honey, could you please pass the potatoes?", which is a loving request. Or you could say in a loud or flat tone, "Pass me the potatoes," which will leave the other person feeling as though he had done something wrong–as if he were IT.

Literally every interaction you have is an opportunity to tell the people in your life that you are glad to have them in your life. And every interaction in which you do not take advantage of this opportunity will result in those people feeling judged and unloved–a sure-fire way to start a TAG-playing conversation.

5.) the way you talk (or don't talk) **about people who are not present**

Your statements about people who are not present can leave a person who is present feeling judged. If you tell your child that you are disgusted by the music that someone else is playing and your child likes that type of music, how can he not feel judged? Even if your critical comments are in no way related to your listener, they still alert him to the fact that you are not safe because you play TAG. And that knowledge will have a very limiting effect upon your relationship with the listener.

Similarly, a lack of positive comments about others (i.e., the passive way of judging those who are not present) will also limit the relationship. If you do not model these sorts of positive comments, the people who are present (especially the young people) won't make them, either. And so the two of you will soon find that you have very little to talk about.

6.) the way that you talk to yourself

If you make a mistake and say out loud, "That was so stupid of me" or some other self-condemning statement, how will others not feel judged (by themselves and by you) when they make a similar mistake? As this example illustrates, every form of TAG is detrimental to the people around you and to your relationships with those people.

YOUR ACTUAL ASSIGNMENTS

1.) Remember to do your "precious lists" every day, with the two "twists" that Dr. Scott suggested. (the prayer of gratitude that procedes the list and the affirmation that follows the list)

2.) Record below all of the data you can remember from two "bad" conversations.

A.) In the first TAG-playing interaction I noticed:

i.) The situation at the time was:

ii.) The things that were said (especially by me) included:

iii.) The emotions that I experienced included:

B.) In the second TAG-playing interaction I noticed:

i.) The situation at that time was:

ii.) The things that were said (especially by me) included:

iii.) The emotions that I experienced included:

CHAPTER 4:

The Alternative to the Game: Choosing Love

"Well, how did your homework assignments go?" asked Dr. Scott.

Elizabeth smiled and said, "We had a lot of fun with the precious lists. The 'I'm so grateful to have you in my life' part was an especially nice addition."

"Good," Dr. Scott encouraged. "Keep that up."

"Oh, we will," she responded. "We also took your 'Plan B' advice and your 'vary the presentation' advice seriously and that worked great. We talked every day and made up different ways to do it each time."

"Hey, way to be creative!" he exclaimed.

Elizabeth smiled. "Once we even involved the kids. They loved being a part of it. In fact, they were really good at it."

Dr. Scott nodded and replied, "Yes, children start with the assumption that they are precious and so they don't think it's weird to hear or to say such things. In fact, they know that it's weird and even hurtful not to hear and say those things."

"That's really true," Elizabeth agreed. "There isn't a day that goes by that my kids don't hug me or show their love for me in some way."

"Right," Dr. Scott affirmed. "And there isn't a day that goes by that they don't just naturally expect to receive that same sort of love from you–the kind of love that lets them know they are special."

Elizabeth said thoughtfully, "So, really, our task is to be more like them."

Dr. Scott replied, "Yes, I believe that Jesus meant it literally when he said in Mark 10 that 'whoever does not enter the Kingdom of God as a child shall not enter it.' If we are willing to learn from them, our children will teach us everything we need to know about choosing love."

Joe impatiently interrupted, "Doctor, Elizabeth is right. The process of sharing our precious lists was a big success. In fact, this week we made love for the first time in a long time, so I know that things are indeed changing for the better."

"But . . ."

"But the 'unhelpful patterns' assignment was really difficult for me," Joe acknowledged, somewhat shamefully.

"Why do you say that?" asked Dr. Scott.

Joe shook his head in frustration. "Once I started paying attention to those patterns, I began to see just how often we fell into them. I saw us playing TAG at least a dozen times a day and I began to get really discouraged."

"Okay."

"Plus," Joe continued, "it was difficult for me to notice those patterns without being judgmental of Elizabeth–without wanting to make her IT in my head."

"Wow, way to go!" exclaimed Dr. Scott proudly.

"Are you being sarcastic, doctor?" Joe wondered.

"Not in the least. I am absolutely, totally impressed with what you've said."

Joe looked puzzled. "In what way?"

"Actually, in two ways. First, you saw very clearly the degree to which the two of you play TAG. That will help to prevent denial from creeping in and undermining your progress."

"What do you mean?"

Dr. Scott explained by saying, "There are lots of people who want to pretend that they don't play TAG–who want to deny what's happening. And since they won't acknowledge the problem, they don't bother to develop the skills that it would take to solve it–skills that I easily could teach them, if only they were willing to learn."

"That must be frustrating for you," Elizabeth interjected.

"Thank you for your compassion," responded Dr. Scott. "Actually, it mostly makes me sad for them. They continue to experience high levels of pain and loneliness and it's all so unnecessary."

"What was your second reason for saying that you were impressed with what I said?" asked Joe.

"I was also impressed with the fact that you noticed yourself playing TAG in your head–that you saw yourself trying to blame the unhelpful patterns you observed on Elizabeth."

"What is so impressive about the fact that I was blaming her?" Joe asked, clearly skeptical.

"Not that you were blaming her. That you noticed yourself doing it," he corrected Joe.

Joe shook his head. "I lost you."

Dr. Scott elaborated, saying, "Most people who find it hard to quit playing TAG find it hard because they think that their attempts at blaming the other person are actually the truth. They want to believe the other person really IS 'the bad one.' But you saw yourself wanting to believe that

Elizabeth was the bad one and you knew that it was a lie. That's a huge step forward."

"So my discouragement and my tendencies to blame Elizabeth prove that I'm actually a TAG genius?" Joe asked, teasing the doctor.

"Well, I'm not sure that the genius label applies, but I am truly pleased to see how much you've already learned in these past couple of weeks."

"Ah, shucks, it was nothing," Joe responded, pretending to be shy.

Dr. Scott smiled. "Actually, that's true."

Joe was a bit taken aback. "Now you are being sarcastic."

"No, I'm actually quite serious."

Joe replied, "I thought you said I had grown a lot. Now you're saying that what I've done is nothing?"

"That nothing is why you've grown," explained Dr. Scott.

"Doctor Scott, you're starting to get a little too weird, even for me."

Dr. Scott just smiled and continued on. "Remember when I talked about planting a seed in the ground and letting it grow?"

Joe nodded and replied, "Yes, you talked about that in the context of talking about how the miraculous growth process would kick in almost automatically, if I would just let go of the fears that previously had kept me paralyzed."

"That's exactly what I meant," responded Dr. Scott. "In the last three weeks, you have stopped pretending that your marriage was okay; you have openly acknowledged how often you play TAG. In other words, you dropped your fear of being transparent. You also have stopped pretending that everything was always Elizabeth's fault–that she was always IT. In other words, you have dropped your fear of being wrong, and because of this, you and your marriage are succeeding greatly."

"So success in relationships actually requires a certain LACK of effort?" asked Joe.

Dr. Scott nodded vigorously. "Oh, yes. Getting it right requires, first and foremost, that we quit working so hard at doing it wrong. Our dysfunctional patterns take a great deal of effort to maintain."

Joe was clearly interested. "In what way?"

Dr. Scott clarified by saying, "We have to be ceaselessly 'proving' to ourselves that we are not wrong, we have to be constantly on guard against attack, and we have to relentlessly push people away, to make sure they don't hurt us. Honestly, it's exhausting to keep doing it wrong."

"That's why I was so tired when we first came in!" Elizabeth exclaimed. "It was because I was spending my energy in the wrong directions–the directions that wear a person out!"

"That's exactly right!" said Dr. Scott, beaming at her.

"Back then, I thought I was tired from working on the relationship."

He smiled. "And you thought the cure was to 'coast' for a while."

Elizabeth nodded. "But you didn't let me get away with that because you knew that in reality I was exhausted from working so hard AGAINST the relationship. And so you pushed me to get serious about our marriage that very day, because you knew that was the only way I was ever going to get un-tired!"

"Precisely," confirmed Dr. Scott. "Now when I ask a client to do something new and they say to me, 'But Dr. Scott, that would be so hard,' I respond by saying, 'There is one thing that would be even harder. Keep doing what you're doing.' I say that because it takes SO much effort to do keep doing it wrong."

"Why is that?" asked Joe

"It's because when we are in wrong relationship, we are literally working against God's powerful will for our lives and when we are in right relationship we are aligned with that awesome power," explained Dr. Scott.

Joe slowly nodded his head. "So the right way is always the easiest way."

"Yes," said Dr. Scott, "because the right way is to choose love and love is always the easiest way. In fact, it is our natural state."

"Love is our natural state?" Joe looked doubtful. "Then why do we have to work so hard to learn it?"

"We don't. We have to work hard to unlearn TAG. As soon as we quit doing that, love reappears immediately."

Joe wanted to be sure he was understanding Dr. Scott correctly. "So love is what we do instinctively once we quit playing TAG?"

"Sure," replied Dr. Scott. "Like I was saying before, love is what every child knows and does effortlessly from Day 1. And it's what we do, too, once we get our thinking straight by remembering God's truth about who we are. As soon as we quit actively or passively pushing people away, what we notice is that we actually love every one of the people in our lives with our whole heart."

"Dr. Scott, are you sure that's true?" asked Elizabeth. "It seems sort of Pollyannaish to think that I love everyone and that everyone loves me. And it seems sort of egotistical too."

He gently chided her, saying, "Only because you're making the mistake of assuming that it's about you."

"What do you mean?" she asked.

"Does the force of gravity only work to pull together 'good' stars and planets?"

"No, of course not," she responded, as if speaking to a child. "The Law of Gravity applies everywhere–it connects every object in the universe to every other object."

Dr. Scott smiled and exclaimed, "Exactly! And 'The Law of Love' works in the same way. God's love is the most powerful force in the universe and it connects all people–in fact, all living things–to one another.

That's why it says in I John 4 that God is love and why Paul, speaking in Colossians 3, says that love is that which binds together all living things. So, what is God? God is that unspeakably powerful force of love that binds together all living things. We are each connected, one to another, heart to heart, by God's love."

Elizabeth thought carefully and said, "So I'm not connected to people because I'm special or because I somehow have deserved it or earned it. I'm connected because everyone is connected through God's love. That's why you said it's not about me?"

"Joe was right–you really are a very clear thinker."

Elizabeth smiled at Dr. Scott. "Thanks. And as you said before, I'm getting even better at it."

"I'm sure you are," Dr. Scott affirmed. "As you so eloquently pointed out, we are all used to thinking about love wrongly–as a bond that connects us to only a few special others and as something we have to earn. In truth, we are all connected by God's love and that love is a free gift, not a prize to be won. Our job is to accept the gift, not to earn the prize."

"So I don't have to make myself love another person," responded Elizabeth. "I already am connected to them by the power of God's love, which binds together all living things."

Dr. Scott nodded. "Right. All you have to do to experience the love you have for the person in front of you is to quit judging them and to quit using those judgments as an excuse to push them away. In other words, as soon as you quit playing TAG against me, as soon as you quit making me the bad one in your mind, you immediately experience your connection to me."

Elizabeth's face clearly revealed her doubts. "Is it really that simple?"

"Yes, and here's your proof. The instant the two of you stopped playing TAG and read your precious lists to each other instead, what happened?"

"I started to fall back in love with Joe immediately."

"Right. Because as soon as we quit playing the game, we experience the real world—a world filled with the loving connections created by our God."

Elizabeth was delighted. "So whenever I say that I love someone, I am telling the truth."

Dr. Scott agreed. "Yes, I meant it when I said that loving one another is our natural state and that we were created by God to be in right relationship. We are so geared to be connected that we literally have to work at not being in right relationship. As soon as we quit pushing love away, the connection shows up again instantaneously."

"Because it never really goes away," Elizabeth responded, checking her understanding.

"Exactly," confirmed Dr. Scott. "That's what the scriptures mean when they talk about God's steadfast love. It means the Law of Love is always in force. So in order to keep ourselves locked into a dysfunctional, unloving pattern, we have to fight off love every minute of every day. It's like pushing a piece of cork underwater. In order for it to stay under, we have to force it to do so, every minute. The instant we quit forcing it down, it pops right back to the surface."

She simply nodded. "And the love we have for people is just like that cork."

"Right," confirmed Dr. Scott. "We are deeply connected to all of the people in our lives and as soon as we quit actively pushing that connection away, it pops right back up. We literally were born to be in loving relationships."

Joe couldn't help teasing Dr. Scott. "So for years now, you have been getting credit for helping all of these couples learn how to love one another and really they already know how."

Dr. Scott joked back, "That's true, but please don't tell anybody. I'm not ready to retire yet."

Elizabeth smiled at their banter but remained uncertain. "Dr. Scott, I want with my whole heart to believe what you are saying. But I am having trouble accepting it, especially in light of what our faith says about the world. Is the world really that good a place?"

Dr. Scott nodded, sadly. "It's true that hard things do happen every day. But that's not the point. The point is, no matter what happens to us, we are in it together. TAG says we're alone but that's a lie–a lie that keeps us lonely and tired. The truth is that God's one promise to us is that we are never alone—that we are always connected to Him and, through Him, to one another. Everything that gives our life purpose and meaning is about embracing those connections."

Elizabeth paused to gather her thoughts, and then said slowly, "So TAG encourages us to push people away, which wastes our energy, keeps us from experiencing God's love, and prevents us from discovering our purpose in life."

"Right, all three times. You are beginning to see, I suspect, why as a Marriage Educator and as a Christian I have made it my life's work to help people to quit playing TAG. The game is incredibly destructive to our faith, our relationships, and our sense of calling."

She replied, "So the incredibly destructive lie is that I am always alone. And the truth is that I could be connected to anyone?"

Dr. Scott clarified, "Not just that you could be–that you are."

"Really? I already am connected to everyone?"

"Sure," said Dr. Scott. "When you read in the newspaper that some other mother's child was lost for two days and has now been found, do you rejoice for that mom?"

"Of course," she replied immediately.

"Even though you have never met her?" he asked.

"Yes."

"Even if she might be from a different country–a country that we regard as our enemy?" he continued.

"Yes," Elizabeth said simply.

"See what I mean?" asked Dr. Scott. "We are connected to everybody right this instant through the power of God's love."

Elizabeth stared at him thoughtfully.

Dr. Scott paused, then continued. "A minute ago you mentioned our faith. What does our faith command that you do?"

Elizabeth responded, "Our faith commands us to love one another."

"To love only certain people?" quizzed Dr. Scott.

"No, to love everyone—even our enemies," she replied.

Dr. Scott nodded. "Right. That's how you can be sure that what I am saying is true. Otherwise, that commandment would be impossible to fulfill."

Elizabeth said, with a note of wonderment, "So, we really DO love everyone. That's what's real."

Dr. Scott shivered involuntarily. "That was so beautiful and so true. God's love connects us to Him and to all people. That's the truth. That's what's real."

Elizabeth continued. "So all of the love we need already exists and already connects us to one another. That's why we are certain to experience love, as soon as we quit fighting against it."

Dr. Scott agreed. "Yes, and it also is why living in right relationship is actually the easiest way to live. What could possibly be easier than simply receiving the sacred love people already have for you and sharing with them the holy love you already have for them?"

"It sounds too easy," Joe commented.

Dr. Scott leaned forward and spoke with great conviction, "It's so easy, even a kid could do it. In fact, that's what every kid does do!"

Joe shook his head. "Why don't the rest of us do it if it's so easy?"

"Again, fear. We are afraid of getting hurt and so we tell ourselves that the safest thing to do is to 'protect ourselves' from getting hurt. And so, instead of choosing intimacy we choose to keep everybody at a distance–by lashing out or withdrawing. We let go of the possibility of experiencing God's miraculous love in order to stay 'safe.' "

Joe looked puzzled. "Why do you say the word 'safe' with such disgust?"

"Because the terrible joke is that as soon as we choose to play the game we become terribly unsafe."

"What do you mean, unsafe?" Joe asked, in his usual clarifying way.

Dr. Scott responded by saying, "Well, the statistics are quite clear. People who play TAG–who use judgment and criticism or silence to keep people at a distance–are more likely to struggle with loneliness, divorce, poor or even no relationships with their children, high levels of stress, physical illness, low productivity at work, and unhappiness–sometimes even to the point of suicide."

"Wow," replied Joe, clearly impressed. "So the things that people do to keep themselves 'safe' actually put them at great risk."

Dr. Scott nodded. "Yes, in every possible way."

"And so if we want to be truly safe, what can we do?" asked Joe.

"The exact three things TAG would tell us not to do. We must put aside the fears that drive our isolation and instead embrace our sacred connections. We must replace our repetitive but comforting interactions with the almost frightening awareness of just how radically open our future really is, once we choose to align ourselves with God's transforming power. And we must choose to tap into that amazing power, instead of telling ourselves that we are powerless victims."

Joe responded, "And how does this relate to the 'noticing unhelpful patterns' homework assignment from this past week?"

Dr. Scott said, "Good question. You are going to use that assignment in a way that will help you to make the three changes I just mentioned. You will have the opportunity to choose connection over isolation, to discover your radically open future, and to embrace empowerment, rather than victimhood. And in the process you will have the opportunity to experience God's love for you in a direct and powerful way."

"Sounds great!" replied Joe, with real enthusiasm. "Where do we start?"

Dr. Scott, looking very serious, said, "First I just want you to more fully understand the reasons behind each of the three changes I will be asking you to make. I want you to see clearly the awful consequences we reap when we choose to play TAG (fear) and the incredible rewards we receive when we choose love instead."

"Okay," Joe asked, "What are the awful consequences of choosing fear and what are the incredible rewards of choosing love?"

"The first awful consequence of TAG is this: when we act as if we are isolated rather than connected, we end up displaying a shocking lack of concern for others. In TAG, we are so busy creating distance, so concerned with 'protecting' ourselves, that we don't even notice the fact that we are hurting everyone else in the process."

Elizabeth wrinkled her brow and asked, "How could people act that way–how could they keep hurting others just to protect themselves? Do people really do that?"

Dr. Scott turned to face her directly. "Well, let me ask you this. When you and Joe were having your destructive arguments in the past, did you ever realize that you were hurting him terribly? And if you ever did notice his pain, did that ever stop you from continuing to hurt him?"

Elizabeth began to weep uncontrollably.

A few moments later, once she had regained her composure, she asked, "Joe, how can you ever forgive me?"

Joe looked incredibly uncomfortable. "I wasn't any better, babe. I made the flip side of the same mistakes."

Dr. Scott gently said, "It doesn't matter what you did in the past. What does matter is that you choose to do it differently—that you learn the lesson. "

Elizabeth replied, "Now that I know, I can never go back. I want with my whole heart to do it differently."

"Good for you," encouraged Dr. Scott. "Your next assignment will be an experience of doing it differently. You will be choosing to be connected–to be an intimate team–instead of choosing to be isolated. And in that process of honoring your connection to one another you will experience great compassion for one another."

Elizabeth wondered, "How is it even possible to interact in a way that is so completely different from our old way?"

Dr. Scott smiled. "Remember, the right way is always the easiest way. I am going to help you to have a 'difficult' conversation that will actually be the easiest one you've ever had."

"I look forward to that," she replied.

"Good. In the instant that you choose to be a team, you will notice that you care deeply about Joe—that the two of you are indeed connected, just as we have discussed. And you will realize that the two of you are having an intimate, powerfully connecting conversation–exactly the sort of conversation that TAG players seek always to avoid."

Joe just shook his head in disgust. "Why didn't we ever have those conversations before?"

Dr. Scott replied, "Remember, in the game of TAG, to be vulnerable enough to be intimate is too frightening–totally unsafe. And if you think back to living with your overly critical dad, you'll realize that in that context it was indeed true. Whenever you were open and honest enough to express your dreams or to admit your mistakes, you got nailed."

Joe nodded. "And so I brought that fear into our marriage."

"Exactly. That fear is a big part of your 50%. And now you can let go of that fear because you are with someone who wants to know you, not to condemn you."

Joe started laughing out loud. "That is a powerfully liberating thought–it makes me feel almost giddy."

Dr. Scott just smiled.

Elizabeth said, "So when you are living in a TAG-playing family, where everyone is concerned only with themselves and no one acts out of compassion for others, it makes perfect sense to conclude that the way to keep yourself safe is to keep everyone else at a distance."

Dr. Scott sighed. "Right. That's why in the past you both were so willing to settle for a relationship that was never truly intimate."

Elizabeth winced and said, "Ouch–that was a little too close to home."

"Sorry," replied Dr. Scott. "I was just trying to remind you—that kind of 'safety' is an illusion. It actually sets a person up for every kind of problem that you can imagine, including intense marital discord."

Elizabeth nodded. "Right–it makes us terribly unsafe, as you pointed out."

Dr. Scott continued, saying, "The only way to be truly safe is to embrace your connection to each another and to become a part of a strong, caring team. This next assignment will give you a chance to be a team and to experience the incredible feelings of true safety that flow out of that sense of connectedness. And in the process you will come to understand what I mean when I say that to experience that sort of peace and connectedness is to have a direct experience of God's presence."

Even Joe was obviously impressed. "Wow. At the risk of pointing out the obvious, that alone would make this entire process worthwhile."

Acknowledging Joe's comment with a grin, Dr. Scott replied, "Thanks. And that's just the beginning. The second awful consequence of playing TAG is this: when we play TAG, we end up having the same useless interactions over and over again."

Joe's face tightened. "We know that feeling–it's incredibly frustrating."

Dr. Scott agreed, saying, "Yes, it's frustrating because instead of joyously claiming the radically open future God has in mind for you, you kept getting stuck in your 'nothing ever changes' present. You get trapped in an ugly and useless pattern that repeats itself over and over."

Joe thought for moment and commented, "When you think about it like that, you would think that people would get bored playing TAG."

"Oh, they do," said Dr. Scott. "Playing TAG always leads to a boring life, although the adrenaline it tends to create often obscures that fact."

Elizabeth interjected, "That describes my family perfectly! I didn't realize this until just now, but a big part of why I tended to avoid spending time with them was because I was always bored. Their interactions may have had a lot of drama, but it was always exactly the same old drama over and over again."

"Right," agreed Dr. Scott. "The fact that they were loud and dramatic, as you have said, tended to cover up the fact that nothing new ever really happened."

Elizabeth summarized by saying," So when my family played the loud version of TAG, they settled for a predictable rush of adrenaline, rather than the excitement of a true adventure."

Dr. Scott looked pleased. "Exactly! To play TAG is to settle for an interaction style that, although it may be filled with what I call trauma and drama, is so utterly predictable that it never can lead anywhere that is fun, interesting, exciting, or purposeful. As Joe said, it's boring."

"How will this next homework assignment help us to break that boring pattern?" Joe wondered.

"Thank you for keeping us on track," replied Dr. Scott. "The assignment will allow you to have a conversation you've never had before, which will be a new and interesting experience. In that instant, your boredom will end and your new God-led adventure will begin."

Joe turned towards Elizabeth and stated, "Well, I personally am ready to quit being bored. Are you ready, honey?"

Elizabeth responded instantly. "Yes, I am really ready for us to have a far more interesting life than the one we had before we came to see Dr. Scott—the one God had planned for us all along."

Dr. Scott smiled. "See, that's why I love working with the two of you. You're always so ready to learn."

"I must admit, we do seem to have found a good teacher," said Joe, playing it straight for once.

Elizabeth enthusiastically nodded in agreement.

"I appreciate the compliment," said Dr. Scott humbly.

Joe replied, "You deserve it. And just so that I'm clear, I think you were saying that our next homework assignment will give us an opportunity to break those first two TAG-playing habits, by having a team-building conversation with each another that is truly safe and by giving us a chance to experience a whole different way to interact."

"Joe, I couldn't have said it better myself."

Joe nodded, smiled, and said, "Maybe I should start getting paid for our sessions."

Dr. Scott, teasing him in return, replied, "The rewards you're receiving are immense, are they not?"

"You've got me there, doc. In terms of my life, my faith, and my marriage, I am indeed getting rich in these sessions."

"I'm glad to hear that," responded Dr. Scott. "On a more serious note, Joe, you were right when you described the first two rewards of your next assignment–a love-based conversation that helps you to feel like a team and also allows you to experience the freedom in Christ that we experience once we quit playing TAG. Before I describe the third reward, I would just like to point out that this entire assignment is possible only because the previous things I said about love are true."

Joe clearly understood. "I get that. We are all powerfully connected to one another through God's love, whether we realize it or not. So having a conversation in which we experience that loving connection is indeed a realistic goal."

"Exactly."

Joe continued. "In fact, having that sort of a conversation shouldn't even take all that much effort–we should discover that it's actually the easiest possible way to interact because we are aligning ourselves with God's power instead of fighting against it."

Dr. Scott enthusiastically nodded his agreement. "Right–it's like swimming downstream in a river. Everything gets really easy, once you choose to align yourself with the current."

"We were swimming upstream for a very long time," said Joe sadly.

"That's true," replied Dr. Scott. "So you know what I mean when I say that doing things the wrong way takes far more effort than doing them right."

Elizabeth joined in, saying, "I understand how the Law of Love makes an intimate conversation possible. But I don't understand how it helps us to break free from having the same old interaction patterns."

Dr. Scott turned toward her and said, "It's because love creates possibilities."

Elizabeth shook her head and responded, "I don't understand."

"If your daughter, Sabrina, came to the two of you and said, 'Mom and Dad, I want to learn how to play the violin,' what would you do?"

"We would start looking around for a good violin teacher."

Dr. Scott continued to coach her, saying, "Because you love her, you would search for a way to bring that possibility into being?"

"Yes."

Dr. Scott concluded, "That's what love always does. As soon as we quit playing TAG and become a team, the godly love that now flows unhindered between us begins to create new possibilities. That's why God is the Creator—because that's what love does—it creates."

Elizabeth replied, "So to choose love is to create new possibilities."

"Yes, always. And those new possibilities are the second of the three rewards that I mentioned."

"This is incredibly helpful," Elizabeth said. Then she asked, "Why don't these sorts of things get taught in school?"

Dr. Scott smiled, a bit sadly. "I sometimes wonder that myself."

She nodded and said, "This homework assignment, which is actually an opportunity to experience God's Law of Love in action, will help us to break the cycle of TAG in those two ways: by helping us to be a team, which will allow us to feel truly safe, and by creating the possibility of interacting with each another in a radically different way, which will help us to see life's possibilities."

"That's exactly right," agreed Dr. Scott.

"Didn't you say there would be three rewards that would flow out of this assignment?" asked Joe.

"Yes indeed, Mr. Taskmaster," teased Dr. Scott. "As I said, for your next homework assignment you are to sit with each other and describe to each other the unhelpful patterns that you noticed. As the third way of breaking the TAG cycle, I want each of you to describe only YOUR contribution to those unhelpful patterns."

"Oh, that will be so hard!" wailed Elizabeth.

"Yes, it will indeed take some effort to break your old habits, but remember it's actually much harder and more tiring to keep doing things your old way."

"Yes, I remember," she sighed.

"Good," said Dr. Scott, seeking to encourage her. "You know, in the 12-step program they define insanity as 'doing things the same way you always have and expecting that this time the results will be different'. If you want to stop the insanity, you must do things differently than you have always done them. That's why our God is the God of transformation, not the God of the status quo."

Elizabeth nodded. "Granted. So how will this help to stop the insanity?"

Dr. Scott continued. "The third awful consequence of playing TAG is this: in TAG, everyone wants to see themselves as the powerless victim, so that they can blame someone else for the problem. You will be doing the exact opposite—you will be taking full responsibility for your half of the pattern."

"How is acknowledging my responsibility the opposite of being powerless?" she wondered.

"Well, Elizabeth, if every problem in your marriage is all Joe's fault, then there truly is nothing you can do to solve the problem–you really are powerless. However, as soon as you can see the role that you play, you know what you can do to change things–you have the power to make a difference."

Elizabeth brightened and said, "So claiming our 50% of the problem—seeing the log in our own eye—is not supposed to make us feel shameful or guilty."

Dr. Scott shook his head. "Absolutely not. It's supposed to help you to feel empowered–to put you back in charge of your own life."

"I get that," she responded, "but it stills seems sort of scary to be so honest about my part of the problem."

"Yes, because in TAG to admit a mistake is to invite attack. To acknowledge a mistake is to get treated badly."

Joe cleared his throat and said, "That's why the first goal is to embrace our connection and to be a team. That way we can create a place where it truly is safe—safe enough for us to tell the truth–the truth about ourselves."

"Right," replied Dr. Scott. "When you create an environment which is compassionate and therefore truly safe, you will be able to acknowledge your past mistakes freely, without fear and without having to worry about being made IT."

"How can we make sure to do that?" asked Joe.

Dr. Scott responded, "It will take a conscious effort. Your old ways of responding are so ingrained in you that you can literally do them without thinking. In order to do things differently, you must actually think–you must consciously decide how you want to act."

"I'm with you," Joe replied. "And just so I get it right, what exactly do we need to consciously decide?"

"You each must be absolutely clear in your own mind about The 50-50 Rule and you must consciously choose to align your thinking with that truth at all times. That way you can stay clear about your goal, which is not to be right but to be part of a loving team."

"Got it," Joe said with conviction. "Anything else we should consciously choose to do?"

Dr. Scott paused to think, then said, "Yes, there is. When you are the speaker, you must choose to focus completely on what YOU did that contributed to the unhelpful patterns you noticed. And when you are the listener, you must remember to thank the speaker for their honesty, rather than judging them for their mistakes."

Joe hesitated, then spoke slowly. "Dr. Scott, that all sounds good, but..."

"But what?"

Joe's words came out in a rush. "But what if I can't see what I did wrong? Remember, I told you I had that problem when I first started noticing our patterns–all I could see was what Elizabeth was doing wrong. I wanted to blame her for everything."

Dr. Scott smiled and replied, "I can pretty much guarantee that will happen for both of you, especially when you first start thinking about those old patterns. That's why you each need to look at your part of the patterns very carefully, <u>before</u> you talk to one another."

"And what primarily should we be looking for?"

Dr. Scott thought for a moment, then explained, "Let me go back for a moment to my silly story about the relationship between that compulsive talker guy and the compulsive listener gal. Do you remember the story?"

Joe nodded. "Sure, they met at a party."

"Right," Dr. Scott affirmed. "They were an example I used to illustrate how all of our problems are actually 50-50 propositions. Well, if you just watched that couple for a moment, you wouldn't conclude that they had a 50-50 problem. What would you conclude if you only observed them briefly?"

Joe seemed unclear, so Elizabeth stepped in and said, "You would think he was an egocentric jerk."

"That's exactly right," Dr. Scott affirmed. "You would have to watch the two of them for a longer period of time to notice that, even when he would ask her a question, she wouldn't answer, that even when he would request input she wouldn't provide it, and that even when he would need her to be a true partner, she wouldn't rise to the occasion and be of help to him."

"So her part would be less obvious," concluded Elizabeth.

"Yes. Even though I can guarantee that every couple's problems are 50-50 problems, I can also guarantee that in any situation one person's 50% will be more obvious."

Elizabeth nodded. "So you would have to look harder to see theirs."

"Yes," agreed Dr. Scott, "in part because it would probably be about what they <u>don't</u> do."

Joe interrupted to say, "You lost me on that one, doc. How can not doing something be a problem?"

Dr. Scott smiled and said, "I can see why you were confused by that. Let me give you an example from my own life. My wife, Rose, and I both grew up in families that handled anger poorly. Rose grew up in a family that expressed anger aggressively–in ways that were loud and hurtful. My family, on the other hand, dealt with anger passively by pretending never to be angry."

"The flip side of her weakness!" Elizabeth grinned, in happy recognition of her own insight.

"Right!" replied Dr. Scott, pleased to see that Elizabeth was so pleased with herself. "So early in our relationship, whenever Rose would get angry and address me in some inappropriate way, I would withdraw because I was so uncomfortable with anger, especially when it was expressed so harshly. I told myself that the ensuing hours of silence we experienced were due to Rose's problem with anger. It took me an embarrassingly long time to realize I was an equal part of both the inappropriate arguments and the silence that would inevitably follow."

Joe shook his head. "In what way? I'm still not getting this."

"Hang with me. Rose would bring up a legitimate point, although perhaps in a hurtful or aggressive way. And instead of addressing the issue she had raised or asking her to make her point in a more constructive way, I passively withdrew–I <u>didn't</u> do any of the helpful things that I could have done."

Joe smiled. "So, basically, you ran."

Pretending to flinch, Dr. Scott said, "That's painfully accurate."

"You did say we were supposed to tell the truth in this office," Joe said, grinning broadly.

"I did indeed. Since I would run away, as you said, the issue would never get resolved. That meant that Rose would have to bring it up again at a later date–she would have to be the nag, which left her feeling even more like she was IT."

Joe replied, "Now I get it. And I'll bet that being even more IT made her even more aggressive."

Dr. Scott nodded his head in confirmation. "Precisely. And so I would withdraw even more quickly and this time there would be an even longer period of silence, during which both of us would feel rejected and misunderstood."

"Which just set the two of you up for your next crummy conversation," Joe concluded.

"You're right; you really do get it," replied Dr. Scott. "Unfortunately, that was exactly what happened. The cycle continued on, in part because I didn't have the courage to hold up my end of the conversation–because of what I didn't do. Is that starting to make more sense?"

"I believe so," said Joe, sounding much more confident. "In order to break your half of the cycle, you needed to take action–you needed to stay in the room and either address the subject or acknowledge the fact that the subject was being addressed in a way that was scary to you."

"And the pattern did shift, the instant I started doing those two things," confirmed Dr. Scott.

"I think I've got it straight now."

"Great. Do you both feel clear about your homework assignment?"

Elizabeth nodded decisively and responded, "We are to be loving teammates who create new possibilities by sharing with one another OUR part of whatever patterns we noticed. And if we are having trouble seeing what we contributed to the problem, we should be on the lookout for the things that we didn't do."

Joe added, "Dr. Scott, I can see how this very intimate exercise will start to build the sense of safety, create the possibility of conversing in a new way, and empower us to change. It will help each of us feel like we can start to trust the other person again because there will be no attacks–just an interesting discussion in which we each step up and experience the empowerment that comes from taking responsibility for OUR mistakes."

Dr. Scott was obviously pleased. "Exactly–it is the next step in breaking the TAG cycle. In fact, in this step the two of you are actually getting ready to replace the game with something far better."

Joe smiled in anticipation. "That's an exciting thought–I love how fast this process of yours brings real results."

"I appreciate the feedback," replied Dr. Scott. "Remember to thank the other person for having the courage to tell the truth about their part of that particular pattern. That's a really important part of creating a new pattern of interacting—a pattern based on love and acceptance, rather than fear and judgment."

Joe rose, extended his hand, and said, "Thank you, doctor. We'll get started right away."

"Good luck. I'll see the two of you next week."

SUMMARY OF CHAPTER 4

- Children assume that they are precious. They fully expect to love and be loved.
- Success in adult relationships requires that we have the same child-like expectations.
- We begin to give and receive the kind of love children expect, the instant we quit pushing it away.
- At that moment of simply receiving love, we begin to understand that to live in right relationship is actually the easiest way to interact–it's the simplest and most natural approach. There is literally nothing to it because God's love already connects us.
- This kind of love does not come to us because we are "special." It is a gift, freely given to all who choose to receive it.
- Accepting this abundant love is what makes us safe. It is far easier to deal with both the good times and the bad times, knowing that we are not alone in dealing with them.
- Thus, real safety lies in choosing community–a stark contrast to the isolation that TAG inspires.
- Choosing love always creates new possibilities. It therefore ends forever the boring, repetitive patterns that are associated with playing TAG.
- Once we have created a safe environment, in which new experiences are valued, we find that claiming our 50% of the problem is an empowering experience, not a shameful one.
- If we are not clear what our 50% is, it might be helpful to look for the things that we don't do, instead of just the things we do.

EXERCISE #3

Please look back at the unhelpful patterns you noted in Exercise #2 and ask yourself the question, "What role did I play in all of that?" Remember that it is important to evaluate not only what you did but also what you didn't do.

As you seek to honestly and truly understand your part of the pattern, it will be helpful for you to remember that you are NOT looking for "the one thing that I did wrong." The patterns you are examining undoubtedly consist of at least a half-dozen steps, each of which triggers the next step. Try to see the whole interaction, including the contributions you made at each step along the way.

For example, in the pattern Dr. Scott described involving he and Rose, the steps probably looked something like this:

Dr. Scott is engrossed in an activity.

Rose feels unimportant. Instead of telling Dr. Scott that she would like his attention, she says "You're always too busy for me" (makes him IT).

Instead of lovingly asking what's wrong, Dr. Scott looks confused and asks, "Now what have I done?" in a sharp tone (plays the defensive role in TAG).

Now Rose feels judged (IT) AND unloved. She gets louder and more hurtful, saying things like, "You don't even care about me."

Dr. Scott believes he is being unfairly attacked and feels afraid of Rose's anger. Instead of speaking up, he attempts to end the conversation, calling it "irrational."

Now Rose feels <u>really</u> abandoned and believes Dr. Scott will pay attention to her only if she forces him to. So she raises her voice even further.

Dr. Scott takes this as a sign that he was right to be afraid and withdraws.

Rose's worst abandonment fears are now realized; she tells herself that she really IS alone and she will carry this belief with her into their next interaction.

Similarly, Dr. Scott's most destructive belief (that he must withdraw in order to remain safe) also gets confirmed and he will carry that stronger belief into their next conflictual interaction.

Hopefully, this brief description of the interaction will help to make it clear that you are looking for a series of steps, not "the one thing I did wrong," that the interaction pattern is always a 50-50 proposition, and that it will be possible in the future to break the pattern by altering what you do at any one of the steps along the way.

Okay, go ahead and analyze your part of the patterns you noticed and listen carefully to your partner as they do the same for the patterns that they noticed. Remember to thank the other person each time they claim their half of a pattern.

MY OBSERVATIONS OF MY BEHAVIOR

Interaction Pattern #1

1.) The actions of mine that contributed to the pattern (e.g., speaking louder and louder, changing the tone of my voice, leaving the room, or choosing a poor time or place):

2.) The actions I avoided taking that contributed (e.g., neglecting to share information, not telling the whole truth, not listening carefully, failing to follow through):

3.) The words I used that escalated things or led us off topic: (e.g., starting sentences with "you," blaming the other person, over-generalizing, referring to the past, name-calling):

4.) Words that I didn't use that would have helped the situation (e.g., acknowledging the truth of what they said, saying thank you, apologizing, comforting them):

5.) Emotions that I expressed in unhelpful ways (e.g., using anger to intimidate them, over-reacting, blaming my reactions on them, not speaking until I was ready to blow up):

6.) Emotions that I failed to express (e.g., pretending to be angry when I actually felt hurt, playing TAG instead of acknowledging my feelings, being passive or a victim):

Interaction Pattern #2

1.) The actions of mine that contributed to the pattern (e.g., speaking louder and louder, changing the tone of my voice, leaving the room, or choosing a poor time or place):

2.) The actions I avoided taking that contributed (e.g., neglecting to share information, not telling the whole truth, not listening carefully, failing to follow through):

3.) The words I used that escalated things or led us off topic: (e.g., starting sentences with "you," blaming the other person, over-generalizing, referring to the past, name-calling)

4.) Words I didn't use that would have helped the situation (e.g., acknowledging the truth of what they said, saying thank you, apologizing, comforting them):

5.) Emotions that I expressed in unhelpful ways (e.g., using anger to intimidate them, over-reacting, blaming my reactions on them, not speaking until I was ready to blow up):

6.) Emotions that I failed to express (e.g., pretending to be angry when I actually felt hurt, playing TAG instead of acknowledging my feelings, being passive or a victim):

CHAPTER 5:

Understanding the Patterns of Our Game

"Well, how did your homework go?" asked Dr. Scott.

"We did it, but we didn't do it very well," lamented Elizabeth.

Dr. Scott nodded his encouragement. "What happened?"

"During some parts of the discussion we did as we were supposed to do and those times were great—our best connecting times ever. However, during one part of the conversation we got completely off track and started to play what we now understand to be a form of TAG. It took us a whole day to resolve that argument."

Dr. Scott looked surprised. "Only one argument for only one day? That's terrific!"

"Honestly, Dr. Scott, I can't always tell when you are being sarcastic with me," Elizabeth complained.

Dr. Scott responded, reassuringly, "Trust me–this isn't one of those times. In the past, how often would you have those destructive arguments and how long would it have taken you to truly resolve such an argument once you had gotten completely off track, as you say?"

Elizabeth replied, "Oh, we had those arguments lots of times and afterwards it would have been silent or strained for days–like we were walking on eggshells. And at the end of that time we still would not have resolved anything. We would just have reached the point where we sort of agreed to pretend that nothing had happened."

Dr. Scott nodded. "Now do you understand my point?"

"I think so," Elizabeth replied. "We actually made a lot of progress, I guess. We had some great moments–times when we felt very close to one another. Those were some clear signs of success. But, as you are now pointing out, even the bad moment ended faster and was settled more completely than it ever would have been in the past, which was actually another form of success."

"And in the process," he pointed out, "you developed some better listening and reconciliation skills. Thus, in the future you will have even fewer misunderstandings and those misunderstandings will get settled more and more quickly. Eventually, you will hardly ever argue and the arguments that you do have will get settled in no time at all."

"Is that really possible?" she wondered.

"Your question is actually backwards," he said, trying to fine-tune her thinking.

By this point, Elizabeth was totally confused. "What?"

Dr. Scott elaborated. "The scenario I depicted is not only possible, it's utterly predictable. What are the odds that a person who practices something–something they literally were born to do—will eventually get really good at it, as long as they keep practicing?"

Elizabeth acknowledged his point. "Pretty high, I would guess."

"In fact," he continued, "is there any chance of this not occurring, as long as they continue to practice?"

"I guess not," she admitted.

Dr. Scott concluded by saying, "That's why I said that your question was backwards. The old TAG-playing part of you assumes that life is an endless series of repetitive interactions and that real change is not possible. So you think the logical question to ask is, 'How could we possibly continue to grow as a couple?' But the real question is, 'Given that you are willing to learn about relationships and that God's one wish is to lead every willing person into deeper and deeper relationship with Him and with others, how could you not continue to grow?'"

Elizabeth clapped her hands together. "That is SO encouraging!"

Her enthusiasm made Dr. Scott smile. "I'm glad. It's really important that you understand this point. If a child wants to learn to play basketball, they would probably start by practicing a simple lay-up. If the child does 100 of them, will they be good at it by the end of that time?"

"Yes, they probably would be," agreed Elizabeth.

Dr. Scott continued, "And if they were a naturally athletic child, blessed with many physical gifts, would it be a near certainty?"

"Yes."

"And if they have the world's most perfect teacher, could there be any other result?"

"No, they would grow measurably better at basketball every time they practiced," she agreed.

Dr. Scott pointed at Elizabeth and said, "Well, that's you. You are open and willing to be taught all there is to know about right relationships, you are diligently practicing those basic skills, as child of God you are hard-wired to learn those particular skills, and God is always leading you on the path that will most perfectly teach you those skills. So what are your odds of success?"

"Very, very high," she grinned.

"Right."

Elizabeth was pleased. "You really do help me to see things in a totally different light–to think radically differently."

Dr. Scott nodded in acknowledgment of the compliment and said, "Here's why that's so important. Remember how I said that everything goes in this order: Think, Feel, Do?"

"Yes," she replied. "I found that to be a very clarifying concept."

Dr. Scott continued. "All transformational change begins with the development of a vision that changes our thinking. As long as our thinking remains unchanged, we're pretty much stuck where we are and the only changes we can make are small, fine-tuning sorts of changes."

Elizabeth shook her head. "Joe and I want something a lot bigger than that."

"I believe you do," replied Dr. Scott, "which is why I am spending so much time on this. In order for the two of you to create a truly intimate marriage, you have to radically change the way you think, which means you need to become far more clear about two things."

"And what are those two things, doctor?" asked Joe.

"First, you need to be absolutely clear about the point I have been raising thus far. If you continue to practice, you WILL get better–a lot better. There is simply NO limit to the quality, depth, and power of the relationship the two of you can create together."

Joe said, by way of clarification, "So we shouldn't just hope to get better; we should expect to get better."

"Yes," confirmed Dr. Scott, "and not just a little better. You should literally expect that at some point in the relatively near future you will be getting so good at this marriage thing that you will begin to teach others how to radically improve THEIR marriages."

Joe responded, with joy in his voice, "I've never said it out loud, doctor, but that has always been a dream of mine–to be passionately in love with my wife and then teach other men how to do the same."

"How to be passionately in love with your wife?"

Joe burst out laughing. "You know what I mean."

Smiling, Dr. Scott said, "Yes, I do. And I would point out that, as with any vision, in the instant that we claim it out loud, it begins to come into being."

Joe smiled. "That sounds insightful. What does it mean?"

"Are you already more in love with your wife than you once were?" asked Dr. Scott.

"For sure."

"And have you already started telling some of the other men in your life about the things you are learning?" he prompted Joe.

"I quote you to my friends all the time."

Dr. Scott concluded by saying, "So your vision is already beginning to come into being. See, once you have the courage to claim your vision, you never have to wonder if you will ever achieve it. The instant you claim it, you begin to see it taking shape right in front of you."

"Dr. Scott, you are one interesting man. Other than talking to Elizabeth, our meetings with you are the highlight of my week."

"Glad to hear it. And thanks for the compliment. Soon, that's the sort of thing other people will be saying about you."

Joe looked thrilled. "Really?"

"I guarantee it," said Dr. Scott with total confidence.

Joe beamed and Elizabeth smiled and leaned over to hug him.

"Joe, you're falling down on the job," commented Dr. Scott, with mock seriousness.

"What?"

"Isn't it your job to keep us on track?" wondered Dr. Scott, feigning innocence.

"I do seem to do that," he acknowledged.

Dr. Scott reminded him, "Well, I said that there were two things you had to be clear about, remember?"

Joe threw up his arms. "Okay, okay, so what's the second thing we need to be clear about, doctor?"

"That's better," teased Dr. Scott. "To get back to my little basketball analogy, the first thing to be clear about is that any child who is willing to practice those lay-ups will indeed get better. And the second is this: the mistakes that the child makes along the way don't matter."

Elizabeth frowned. "Joe and I both tend to act like our mistakes DO matter–we get really down on ourselves when we mess up. Sometimes we can get down on each other too."

Dr. Scott nodded. "Yes, I've seen lots of evidence of that. But let's go back to that kid practicing lay-ups. As long as they shoot 100 of them, will they get better?"

Elizabeth looked a bit irritated and replied, "That's what we've been talking about."

"Right," Dr. Scott continued, "but now I want to take that one step further. As long as they continue to shoot those 100 shots, does it matter if they miss the 37th one?"

She shook her head. "Not in the least, as long as they keep practicing."

Dr. Scott looked a bit smug. "Precisely. Now when you came into my office today and said that you had done your homework, I was very pleased. You thought I would be displeased when I heard that you made some mistakes in the process, but I couldn't have cared less about those mistakes."

Elizabeth nodded slowly. "Because you understand that mistakes don't matter–that as long as we keep practicing, we will indeed get good at this thing we are practicing."

"Right," confirmed Dr. Scott. "And because I understand this, too—although our mistakes don't matter—the decision to learn from our mistakes matters terribly."

Joe added, "So, if we get down on ourselves, just because we make mistakes. . ."

"Then you are just like the child who says, 'I missed my 32nd lay-up. Does that mean I am a loser and should quit trying?' That's crazy thinking. A successful person is not someone who never fails. A successful person is someone who takes that 33rd shot, after first reflecting for a moment on the lessons to be learned from having missed the 32nd one."

Joe nodded, decisively. "So we should just keep practicing no matter how many mistakes we make."

"Yes," confirmed Dr. Scott, "and you should keep learning from those mistakes. In the game of TAG your mistakes supposedly 'prove' something about you—that you are stupid, or no good, or can't do anything right. But in reality, they don't mean anything about who you are. They just point out certain lessons that God wants you to learn. Like maybe you need to arch the ball a little higher next time."

"That's SO helpful," Joe replied.

Dr. Scott continued by saying, "Imagine that your daughter, Sabrina, comes home tomorrow and says, 'Dad, I did poorly on my math test. Do you still love me?' You would understand that that was a crazy question, right?"

"Of course," Joe said, vehemently. "Her math grade has nothing to do with my caring for her."

Dr. Scott smiled gently. "In other words, she still would be precious beyond words. Her score would have nothing to do with who she was to you or how important she was to you."

"That's true," remarked Joe. "At most, her poor performance would mean that I needed to help her find a better way to study for math."

"Precisely. Her low test score would say nothing about who she was to you but it would point to a lesson that needed to be learned. Right?"

"Right," replied Joe. "So you will always be pleased when we do our homework and you will never care very much about the fact that we may have made some mistakes in the process, as long as we continue to learn from those mistakes. I'm thinking that God must want us to hear that same message—that He loves us no matter what and that He would want for us to learn from our mistakes, for our sake as well as His."

Dr. Scott beamed. "Exactly. Mistakes were and will continue to be a given. The only question is, 'Will you learn the lessons and continue on, stronger than ever, or will you beat yourself up for your mistakes and quit?' That's what TAG-playing people do. That's why, for them, nothing ever changes."

Elizabeth asked, "Why would they quit when the rewards of learning are so great?"

Dr. Scott explained, "Remember, in TAG it is not important to be right but it is terribly important not to be wrong. Learning a lesson, so as to get something right, is of little importance. Mistakes, on the other hand, are very scary and must be avoided at all costs. So as soon as I make a mistake, I quit."

Elizabeth nodded her head, sadly. "So people who play TAG sacrifice any chance at happiness, fulfillment, and right relationship, just to avoid being wrong."

"You have just summed up the entire problem with TAG in one sentence," replied Dr. Scott.

Joe said, with obvious pride, "I told you she was great at that."

Elizabeth blushed and smiled shyly at Joe.

Dr. Scott smiled and commented, "Indeed you did. Do the two of you understand the power of what just happened?"

Seeing their puzzled looks, Dr. Scott continued, "The two of you just had a momentary experience of the anti-TAG."

Joe laughed and said, "Okay, I'll bite–what's the anti-TAG?"

"In TAG, I look for everything you do wrong–for the '10' part of The 90-10 Rule. I use those mistakes against you to make you IT, thereby confirming to both of us that we are indeed on opposite sides. The inevitable results of such an experience are isolation, loneliness, and despair.

Joe looked grim. "Been there, done that."

Dr. Scott continued, "But, in the anti-TAG, I look for what you do right and I celebrate that, which gives us a chance to experience the truth that we are powerfully connected through God's love. The result of that experience is always an increased sense of love and a joy that sort of bubbles out of us."

Elizabeth interjected, "That IS how I felt at that moment–overjoyed."

Joe replied, "And I DID feel very in love–like we were totally connected in that instant."

Dr. Scott pointed at them both and said, "Thanks to God, you were and are. And now you know what we're aiming at. The goal is sanctification—for the two of you to continue to have that sort of sacred, anti-TAG experience, a higher and higher percentage of the time."

"Is it possible to feel that way all of the time?" Elizabeth wondered.

Dr. Scott shrugged, saying, "Well, I am still very much on the journey myself. But I can tell you that I have gotten to the point where I now feel that way a lot of the time. And since God's love is constant, it should be possible to experience it all of the time."

Elizabeth beamed. "That gives us something to shoot for, doesn't it, Joe?"

Joe nodded but looked uncertain.

"What's the matter, Joe?" asked Dr. Scott, with a note of concern in his voice.

"Well, this is all very interesting and sort of uplifting, but I feel like we have wandered a mile away from what we are supposed to be talking about and from our homework assignment. I don't want to be critical but I don't want us to waste our time either."

Dr. Scott put his hand on Joe's shoulder and said, "Joe, just like you don't have to worry about being made IT during our sessions, you don't have to worry about making me IT either. Anytime you have a concern, you can voice it and I never will take it as an attack."

Joe, obviously relieved, said simply, "Thanks, doc."

"And as for the homework assignment, we are now ready to discuss it. I just wanted to make sure, first, that our discussion would be maximally helpful."

Elizabeth put her hand on Joe's knee to comfort him and then turned toward Dr. Scott. "What does it take for the discussion to be maximally helpful?"

"It takes three things. First, the discussion needs to take place in the context of being pleased and proud that you did the assignment. What makes a particular action praiseworthy is not the result of the act but rather the act itself–in this case, the fact that you summoned up your courage and did the assignment, despite the fact that it was outside of your comfort zone. That took guts and a clear decision to choose love over fear."

Elizabeth understood. "So instead of being critical of the fact that we weren't very good at it, we should be pleased that we did the assignment at all, being clear in our minds that as long as we keep doing the assignments, we will indeed get very good at this process."

"Bingo. The second factor is the reason I made such a big deal of the fact that you experienced the anti-TAG a moment ago. In order for our conversation about your homework assignment to be maximally effective, the two of you must focus almost exclusively on what you did RIGHT. The knee-jerk reaction of any former TAG-player is to focus on their mistakes. But the data is quite clear; we actually learn way faster and far more perfectly by focusing on what we do right and by building on our strengths."

"I noticed that you have yet to ask us about one thing we did wrong," Elizabeth commented.

"Yes," affirmed Dr. Scott, "and now you know the reason. I did not want to start the conversation there because it's simply not helpful to have that be our starting point."

Elizabeth summarized by saying, "So the second thing we have to do in order for our upcoming discussion to be maximally effective, is to focus on what we did right while we were doing our assignment."

"Yes, to focus on what you did right, so as to develop a clear mental picture of the goal—a vision that can guide your new way of thinking. That's why I talked about your anti-TAG experience a moment ago. I did it to help you to develop that clear picture—that vision. Because once you have a clear vision . . ."

Joe jumped in, "It immediately starts coming into being!"

Dr. Scott smiled. "You guys are so fun to work with."

"Is it a joy?" teased Elizabeth.

Dr. Scott turned serious. "In fact, it is. Any experience of connecting creates joy and so when I have the experience of connecting with my clients, like the three of us did just a second ago, it is indeed a joyful moment."

Elizabeth beamed. "I'm pleased that it's as fun for you as it is for us."

"Thanks," replied Dr. Scott. "That brings me to the third factor–the third thing that has to be true in order for our conversation about your assignment to be maximally effective."

"And what is that third factor?" wondered Elizabeth.

"The third factor is this. In the context of being proud that you did the assignment and in the process of developing a clear vision, we will talk about your mistakes only in terms of 'what is the lesson–what do I need to learn from this mistake, in order to bring me closer to the vision?' Do you understand?"

"Sure—we will need to be like the kid who knows he just has to arch the ball a little higher in order to make a basket," she replied.

"Right–there must be no playing TAG–no attacking yourselves or the other person for making mistakes," cautioned Dr. Scott. "Just a willingness to ask, 'What does this teach us?' and to take those lessons to heart, so that your mutual vision comes one step closer to being your reality."

Elizabeth smiled. "This will be a very different conversation than anything we've ever had."

Joe asked hesitantly, "What if we are not able to do that very well?"

Dr. Scott replied, "That's like asking, 'What if we don't do our homework assignment perfectly?' And what do you suppose would be my answer to that question?"

Elizabeth jumped in. "I think I am beginning to understand the way that you think. You would think, 'Well, of course you won't do it perfectly,' and you wouldn't even care about that. You would just be glad that we were trying, you would ask that we focus on what we did well, and you would help us to learn whatever lessons we might need to learn from our mistakes. Did I get it right?"

Dr. Scott, with a twinkle in his eye, replied, "So right, it's almost scary."

Joe added, "I'm really starting to see what you meant, doctor, about how I always assume that I'm going to be IT. And you're right. It doesn't matter if we do this next conversation perfectly. In fact, we won't. And so what! As long as we practice, develop a clear vision, and learn the lessons that will bring us closer to that vision, eventually we will get better at this sort of conversation. In fact, we will get to be really good at it—so good that we will then teach it to others."

Dr. Scott smiled gently and nodded. "And your teaching will be very effective, because your listeners will be able to tell that you have been where they are and have been transformed by God's love. You will be a sign of hope for them."

Joe was almost afraid to wish for that. "I want that with my whole heart."

Dr. Scott waved his hand theatrically, "And it shall be so."

"How can you be so sure that my vision will come true?" Joe asked skeptically.

Dr. Scott responded, more seriously, "Because it is already starting. And because now you won't rest until it comes true. Right?"

"Right. Let's get started. I honestly don't want to waste a second, now that I know where we're going."

"Great," replied Dr. Scott. "Let's talk about your homework experience, in which you discussed the times that you played TAG and the role that you played in each of those games."

Joe said, "I'll start."

Dr. Scott nodded and reminded him, "I want to hear what went right first."

"Well, to begin with," Joe replied, "we did indeed do the assignment, which I now understand is the most important thing of all. And I was able to identify two things I have often done in the past that frequently have triggered the game of TAG between the two of us."

Dr. Scott was pleased. "Very impressive–that's a huge accomplishment. Remember, once you truly understand a pattern the solution will become obvious. So I meant it when I said that I was impressed. What were the two things you noticed yourself doing?"

Joe replied, "First, I was too quick to respond–oftentimes, I reacted even before Elizabeth was finished speaking. That left her feeling like I wasn't really listening to her and like she was not important to me."

Dr. Scott nodded. "That's the game I call Rehearsal. When I am supposed to be listening I am actually composing my answer, which I then insert into the 'conversation' as soon as I can."

"Yeah, that's what I do," confirmed Joe.

Dr. Scott replied, "Just so you're clear, it's not quite accurate to say that the game leaves Elizabeth 'feeling' like you aren't listening."

Joe looked confused. "What?"

Dr. Scott continued, "It's not a feeling; it's a fact."

Joe laughed. "That's true. When I'm rehearsing, as you say, I am not totally listening to what Elizabeth is saying."

"Actually, you're not listening at all."

"Golly, nail me, why don't you!" Joe exclaimed.

Dr. Scott pointed out, "In TAG, it is really scary to admit our mistakes, as I have said. So when acknowledging a mistake, the tendency is to soft peddle it or to downplay it–anything to avoid completely owning up to our mistakes."

"I can see that in myself," Joe said.

"So part of recovering from that fear-based mindset is to get better at naming our mistakes, with no qualifiers—just like in a confessional. That way, we find out that we can make mistakes and still be loved–that our mistakes don't 'prove' we are bad, or IT, or unlovable."

Joe nodded. "Okay, so one of the things I learned in analyzing our old TAG conversations, is that I sometimes play Rehearsal, which prevents me from listening to Elizabeth."

"Beautiful."

Joe continued, "And it also sends her the message that she is not important to me."

Dr. Scott smiled broadly. "I'm proud of you. No spin, no rationalization, and no qualifiers–just the truth."

"Gosh, I thought it would make me feel bad to admit my mistakes so openly," Joe replied excitedly. "But it doesn't. In fact, it makes me feel good, if that's possible. Like I'm free."

"You are free," confirmed Dr. Scott. "You just experienced true freedom in Christ—the freedom that comes from knowing you are precious, regardless of your behavior. 'For I am the truth and the truth shall set you free.' Now you are truly free."

"Like my daughter, Sabrina, is free when she finds out that I love her dearly, even on the days when she flunks her math test?"

"Exactly," affirmed Dr. Scott. "In the crazy, pretend world of TAG, everything is conditional. In the world God actually created, everything that matters is constant. And it's incredibly freeing to find that out."

Joe said hesitantly, "You mean Elizabeth won't think less of me now that I have openly admitted to the first of my two frequent mistakes?"

"I'm guessing that she's proud of you, not ashamed of you. Let's ask her."

Elizabeth responded immediately. "Dr. Scott is right. I am very proud of you. And I felt closer to you the instant you said that your Rehearsal behavior made me feel unimportant. I could tell in that transparent moment that you actually got it—you really did understand the game's impact upon me. And when I could tell you understood me, I felt cared about by you and more in love with you. It was great."

Joe grinned. "Wow, I'm going to have to start making even more mistakes."

Dr. Scott smiled back at him. "Or, at least, you are going to want to start getting better at acknowledging the mistakes you already made."

"Point taken."

Dr. Scott asked, "Is there anything else you want to say abut this topic before we move on to the second big insight you had about yourself, Joe?"

"Well, I guess I do have one last question. Now that I have fully acknowledged the ways in which my playing Rehearsal have hurt Elizabeth, I feel really bad. Is that just a sign that I'm beating myself up–that I am making myself IT?"

Dr. Scott shook his head. "No, it's a sign of something I always say. The instant I quit playing TAG, my fear is replaced with compassion."

Joe nodded thoughtfully. "So that silly cork analogy you used is actually true."

"See how smart you are?" affirmed Dr. Scott. "Yes, the instant I quit using TAG to push people away, I experience our connection and in the context of that sacred connection, what I feel is compassion. So if I have hurt another person, I will indeed feel bad for them. Not bad about myself–not bad like I am IT. Bad for them because they have been hurt. Do you understand the difference?"

"Totally. I feel bad, on her behalf, and I want her life to be better," Joe replied.

"Exactly," said Dr. Scott. "In TAG, I am so busy trying not to be IT myself, so self-centeredly caught up in my own fear, that I literally don't even see the hurt I cause others. But as soon as I stop playing, I see that hurt all too clearly and I truly feel badly about it."

Joe grimaced. "How do I get rid of that feeling?"

"You don't get rid of it–you use it," replied Dr. Scott.

"Use it for what?" Joe asked.

Dr. Scott prompted him. "When you acknowledge the hurt you have caused Elizabeth and you experience your compassion for her, what does it make you want to do?"

Joe thought for a moment and then responded, "It makes me want to be a better man and a better husband. It makes me want to be different–totally different. It makes me even more determined to become the man that God created me to be."

Dr. Scott nodded. "Precisely. Our simple acknowledgment of the truth always leads to change. It is the most powerful motivational tool in the world. That's why the truth does indeed set you free. In TAG, nobody ever acknowledges the truth and so nothing ever changes–you see the same old patterns over and over again. In the real world, where people tell the truth without fear, change is constantly occurring. That's why I always say that our God is a God of transformation."

"And that's also why you said there's no limit as to how great our marriage can become–because with God's love flowing freely through us, change will be constantly occurring and so our marriage will keep getting better and better all of the time."

"Right," affirmed Dr. Scott. "Every day you will grow closer and closer to each another—the two shall become more and more as one. And in twenty years, that will be just as true as it is today," replied Dr. Scott.

Joe's eyes grew wide. "That's incredible. What a God! And what a vision!"

Dr. Scott agreed, then prompted, "And now that you have that vision. . ."

". . .I realize that it is already beginning to come true right before my eyes. And it IS! This is SO great; Elizabeth and I are going to have an incredible marriage!"

"And soon you will be teaching others."

"Dr. Scott, you are one inspiring man."

Dr. Scott smiled in response. "Thanks. Let's keep moving. You said there were two mistakes that you noticed. The first was the tendency to play Rehearsal. What was the second one?"

Joe replied, "I realized that I often had sort of a chip on my shoulder before we even started, which caused me to get defensive at times when Elizabeth was just trying to make conversation."

Dr. Scott nodded. "That's what I meant before, when I talked to you about always assuming you were going to be IT. I call that game

Victim, because we play it when we are afraid we are going to be the victim in the conversation–when we are anticipating being made IT."

Joe clearly understood. "Yeah, I noticed I was especially likely to act that way when we were addressing a topic I thought might lead to a conflict."

"I'm guessing that's when you are most likely to play Rehearsal too," Dr. Scott remarked.

After a moment of reflection, Joe responded, "I hadn't thought about that, but now that you mention it, I'm sure you're right. How did you know that?"

Dr. Scott grinned. "Because I'm psychic. Seriously, if you think about it, it makes perfect sense. Those two games, Rehearsal and Victim, almost always go together. If I think you're going to attack me, then I start putting together in my head all of the reasons why I shouldn't be IT."

Joe nodded. "In other words, as soon as I feel like the Victim, I kick into Rehearsal mode."

"Right," confirmed the doctor. "And what is the purpose of Rehearsal mode?"

"To prove that I'm not IT."

Dr. Scott asked, "And in TAG, what is the only way for you not to be IT?"

Joe responded, "To make the other person IT."

"So as soon you fear that you are about to become the victim, you start rehearsing, which means you are actively trying to prove to Elizabeth that she is IT–that she is the bad one, the unlovable one, the one who deserves to be treated poorly."

Joe grimaced, nodded his head slowly, and said, "Yes, I guess that's right."

Dr. Scott continued, "And so how do you suppose the process leaves her feeling?"

Joe hung his head. "Terrible about herself; like she's worthless."

"Elizabeth, is that right?" asked Dr. Scott.

Elizabeth looked both angry and sad. "That is so right, I want to start yelling right now! Like 'You have no right to treat me like that!' And I want to cry, too, for that little girl inside of me whose parents kept telling her she was no good."

Joe was clearly shaken. "I never even thought about the fact that my fear of being the victim was so hurtful to you–that it would add to all of the old, destructive messages you received when you were a girl. I feel awful."

Dr. Scott prompted him. "Right–and that feeling makes you want to…"

"Change, starting right now," Joe said with conviction.

"Right. So tell her."

Joe turned toward Elizabeth and said, clearly and powerfully, "Honey, you are SO precious to me. I want to lift you up and to celebrate everything that is great about you, not be just one more person who tears you down. I commit myself to breaking that old pattern, starting right now. As of today, you will always know you are precious to me."

Elizabeth said simply, "You're my hero."

Dr. Scott teared up. "You know, lots of people say things to me like, 'Dr. Scott, it must be really depressing to do your job–it must be really hard to be constantly in the presence of people with problems.' They don't get it–I get to see miracles in my office every day."

Elizabeth and Joe nodded, fighting back tears of their own.

Dr. Scott continued. "People think going to therapy means admitting you have problems. I think going to therapy means you are finally ready to let God perform a miracle."

After a long pause, Elizabeth said, "I couldn't agree with you more, Dr. Scott. I'm ready to keep being a part of this particular miracle. So, is it okay if I talk about the pair of mistakes I have often made?"

"Certainly."

"Well, the first thing I realized was I was constantly trying to fix Joe. Instead of just listening to him when he was telling me about his day at work, for example, I would give him advice that he hadn't asked for, criticize a decision he had made, or tell him how he should have handled the situation."

Dr. Scott nodded and said, "I'm guessing, Joe, that her Fixer mode left you feeling like, 'I don't want to talk about work anymore.' Is that true?"

Joe looked sad and said, "Yes, I always just wanted to be understood—to have Elizabeth be a sounding board for me. Eventually, I gave up trying and withdrew into myself."

Dr. Scott prompted him, "And then felt alone and abandoned, I suspect."

Joe agreed. "I wouldn't have thought of those words on my own but, yes, that is true."

Elizabeth jumped in immediately. "But that wasn't my purpose—I didn't mean for you to feel that way!"

Dr. Scott turned to Elizabeth and said, gently and clearly, "You're not IT, you know."

"That's why I reacted that way? Because I felt like I was IT?" she wondered aloud.

"Yes–you thought that you needed to defend yourself, which is a clear sign you believed yourself to be IT. But since you are God's precious child you can't be IT. So there is no need to defend yourself."

"Not ever?" she asked.

"Not ever," Dr. Scott reassured her. "Even if Joe did indeed feel alone and abandoned, what would that mean about you?"

"That God had an important lesson for me to learn?"

"Precisely. And all of your defensiveness and all of your 'explaining' just gets in the way of learning His lesson."

Elizabeth nodded. "So I should just drop the attitude, pay attention, and learn the lesson—exactly what God is always asking us to do."

Dr. Scott smiled. "You are amazing. And you're right. So what is the lesson?"

"That when I tell Joe what to do–when I am playing Fixer or being controlling, as he calls it—I prevent him from getting his needs met, in terms of companionship and clarification. So, in the end, instead of experiencing his connection to me, he feels misunderstood and alone."

"Joe, is that about right?" asked Dr. Scott.

"As usual, Elizabeth nailed it."

Elizabeth commented, "I see what Joe meant about feeling bad and wanting passionately to change. Now that I know what I did to hurt him, I really, really want to be different."

"In what way?" asked Dr. Scott.

"I want to listen instead of playing Fixer, so Joe feels like I really am with him. I want to be his friend, instead of acting like the enemy. I want him to know that he will never be alone again."

"Good for you!" exclaimed Dr. Scott. "Now, here's the great part. Once Joe can tell that you understand the situation and that you are really on his side, he will want to hear your ideas."

Elizabeth looked doubtful. "How do you know that?"

"Didn't you hear him say he wanted to use you as his sounding board?"

"Yes," she acknowledged.

Dr. Scott turned to Joe and asked, "Joe, did you mean that?"

"Absolutely," Joe responded. "I love to talk things through with Elizabeth. I admire the way her mind works and the fact that she always has a different slant on things–a way of looking at the situation that frees me up to be more creative in my approach."

Dr. Scott nodded. "That's what I thought." Turning back toward Elizabeth, he continued, "See here's the deal, Elizabeth. That solution-oriented mind of yours is actually very helpful, but only if you use it in the right order."

"The right order?" she queried.

"Yes. If you take the time to truly understand the situation before you begin to analyze it, you will help Joe to feel cared about, since listening shows caring, and your proposed solutions will be more helpful, since they will be based on a clear understanding of the situation. You will build the relationship AND contribute to a good outcome."

Elizabeth nodded. "Got it."

Dr. Scott continued, "On the other hand, if you start telling Joe what to do before you take the time to listen, three bad things will happen. First, Joe will feel attacked and withdraw from the conversation. Second, your suggestions will be inappropriate and unhelpful, since you don't yet understand the situation. And finally, your TAG-playing fear of mistakes will take over the conversation and the relationship."

"The first two make total sense to me. The last one doesn't yet," Elizabeth replied.

"Thanks for telling me. Let me expand on that one a bit," responded Dr. Scott. "Whenever you react in that Fixer way it is because you are feeling fearful–fearful that Joe will make a mistake and that the 'right' outcome will not occur."

"I believe you."

Dr. Scott continued. "Remember, there are only three main ways of interacting: factual, intimate, and TAG. Ask yourself when you are thinking an obsessive thought, caught up in fear of making a mistake, or acting in your old controlling manner, which of these three types of interactions do you suppose you are having?"

"TAG, for sure," Elizabeth acknowledged.

"Right," confirmed Dr. Scott. "So now here is Joe, thinking he is having a conversation that is partly factual, where he is simply relaying information, and partly intimate, where he is giving you a chance to know him better. Suddenly, without any warning, he is jerked into this TAG interaction. I can assure you, it is both shocking and upsetting to him."

"And then what happens?" Elizabeth asked.

"In that specific conversation, he probably reacts badly and probably feels totally caught off-guard and flustered–like an unsuspecting Victim. In his shock, all he can think about is 'this shouldn't be happening and you shouldn't be treating me like this.' In other words, he makes you IT, at least in his head. And he begins to plan his words more carefully, instead of just being his spontaneous self. And that's the beginning of Rehearsal!"

"Wow!" she exclaimed.

Joe shuddered, "That gives me the chills."

Dr. Scott nodded. "That means that one of the concepts I have been teaching you must suddenly make a lot more sense to you."

"What's that?" Joe asked.

"The 50-50 Rule," responded Dr. Scott.

Joe looked puzzled. "The rule that says that every one of our dysfunctions is a two-way street?"

"Right," affirmed Dr. Scott. "When we were speaking earlier, you correctly noted that you tended to play the two games I call Victim and Rehearsal. But that was only half of the picture. This helps to complete the picture. Instead of saying 'I tend to play Victim and Rehearsal,' it would be more accurate for you to say 'Elizabeth and I have this pattern that we do together. When she gets afraid that I might make a mistake, she tries to resolve her fear by switching into Fixer mode. The judgment I experience when she does that leaves me feeling like I am suddenly IT, which makes me want to defend myself. So instead of listening to her fears, I start to rehearse the arguments I can use to prove to her that she is IT, not me."

Elizabeth said, "That's so accurate, it's scary. But does that mean the TAG game which results is all my fault?"

Dr. Scott shook his head intensely. "No, the 50-50 Rule always applies. In this immediate situation, instead of recognizing your fear and reassuring you, Joe unthinkingly reacts by going immediately into Rehearsal. His reaction leaves you feeling even more alone. That increases your fear, which increases his Rehearsal reaction, and things escalate. That's one level of the 50-50 Rule–the present circumstance.

Here is the second level to which the 50-50 Rule applies. Let's say this interaction ends with Joe withdrawing from the conversation, so that you literally are left alone. When there's a problem tomorrow, what are you going to assume?"

"That I have to solve the problem myself!" she exclaimed.

"Exactly," confirmed Dr. Scott. "And so your Fixer pattern continues, stronger than ever."

Elizabeth stopped to clarify. "So it's always 50-50, both at the present moment and with regards to the future?"

Dr. Scott nodded. "Always. We each play a 50-50 role in the present interaction AND our 50 makes the other person's 50 more likely to happen in the next conversation. That's why the question 'Whose fault is this?' is always a crazy question."

"I understand," said Elizabeth. "My fearful attempts at control make Joe more likely to play Rehearsal, both now and in the future. And his playing Rehearsal makes me more likely to be controlling, both now and in the future."

"Right. So whose fault is it?"

"Dr. Scott, that's a crazy question!"

He simply smiled and said, "You're a quick learner. Here's where it really gets interesting. It's important to understand that the roles we have just described for each of you were your old comfort zones."

"But I never wanted to behave like that," protested Joe.

"Of course you didn't," Dr. Scott reminded him. "Remember, our fearful comfort zones are never what we actually want. They are what we settle for, because they are familiar to us."

Elizabeth interjected, "So acting like I have to solve everything myself, without any in input from others, is my comfort zone? How could anyone pick that as a comfort zone? That way of life would be so lonely."

Dr. Scott shot back, "It was lonely for you–and it left you feeling overwhelmed too. Yet, it was indeed your comfort zone."

Elizabeth acknowledged the truth of his words and shook her head in despair. "Why on earth would I ever pick that?"

In reply, Dr. Scott asked, "In the family you grew up in, what happened when you tried to share your plans or involve others in your dreams?"

"I got a long list of reasons why my idea wouldn't work. And when I tried to involve others, they always failed to follow through on their part. I know now that both their negativity and their procrastination occurred because they were afraid of making a mistake."

Dr. Scott kept coaching her. "What conclusion did you come to, based on that data?"

"That is was better to just be separate and take care of everything myself."

"And ever since. . ." prompted Dr. Scott.

"I have been acting as if I have to take care of everything myself," declared Elizabeth.

"Which leaves Joe feeling. . ."

"Inadequate and probably unnecessary," she acknowledged sadly.

"To which he responded by. . ."

"Getting defensive and being gone a lot. I accused him of being thin-skinned and a workaholic. Now I know why he acted like that." Elizabeth began to cry.

After a pause, Dr. Scott continued. "And Joe, in the family you grew up in, what would happen when you spontaneously shared your thoughts or feelings?"

"I got criticized and ridiculed no end, especially by my dad," Joe responded.

"Which led you to decide . . ."

"Not to share any idea of mine, unless I had first prepared a long list of reasons why it was not a stupid idea."

"And ever since. . ." prompted Dr. Scott.

"Whenever I expected someone to be critical of me (Victim), I went into the Rehearsal mode that you described earlier. I prepared a mental list of reasons why they were wrong to think that way."

"Which left Elizabeth feeling like. . ."

"Like I was not really hearing her concerns, which you pointed out was not a feeling but a fact. And like she was all alone. "

"Which led her to be…"

"The controlling, 'I'll do it myself' Fixer woman that I accused her of becoming," concluded Joe, looking very sad himself.

Dr. Scott summarized by saying, "I'm hoping this part of our conversation helps you each to be clear about four things:

1.) there is no use blaming each other for your dysfunction, since you each came into the marriage with your particular dysfunction–your old, fear-driven comfort zone.

2.) our comfort zones lead to TAG patterns that are destructive in the present and that strengthen the probability that we will continue to play exactly the same game in the future.

3.) each of your behavioral dysfunctions was based on a belief–a belief you developed in childhood, based on the data you had at the time.

4.) you will change your behavior patterns only when you change your beliefs."

Elizabeth wondered, "What beliefs do I need to adopt instead of my old ones?"

"Well, for starters, the belief that being a part of a team is a wonderful thing, the belief that Joe would want nothing more than to meet your needs, if only he knew what they were, and the belief that what you and Joe do is nowhere near as important as doing it together."

"That's a tall order," she responded.

Dr. Scott smiled. "You know what I think about that."

"What?" she asked, not understanding.

"Here's a far, far taller order. Try to be happy without adopting these new beliefs."

Elizabeth nodded, remembering. "The right way is always the easiest way."

"Yup."

"OK," she summarized, "so I can jettison my old beliefs and be happy, or keep my old ones, remain in my comfort zone, and be unhappy."

"Precisely," replied Dr. Scott. "And here's the weird part. Most people choose 'B.' "

"Why on earth would they do that?" she wondered.

"Why did you?" he asked, challenging her thinking.

Elizabeth thought for a moment and said, "In the past, no one supported my ideas or followed through on those times when they claimed to support me, which left me feeling like I must be stupid or naïve. In other words, like I was IT. So the way not to be IT was to trust no one, keep my ideas to myself, and just do everything on my own."

"Why did you keep choosing Option B?" he prompted.

"Because it kept me from being IT," she replied.

"And why are you ready to choose Option A now?" asked Dr. Scott.

Elizabeth answered confidently. "Because now I know that I can't be IT–I am a precious child of God. Because now I know that everything is 50-50. And because now I know there is more to life than fearfully avoiding mistakes. I'm ready to be all the way alive–to have a life and a marriage that is powerful and good, not just un-bad."

Dr. Scott beamed. "Truly, I couldn't be more happy for you."

Joe interjected "Me neither honey. But. . ."

"But what?" she asked.

Joe replied, "Well, there were two things that you talked to me about during our homework assignment and so far you've just talked about the first one–the one where you tell me what to do because you are trying to control everything yourself."

"Right. Dr. Scott, the second mistake I saw myself making a lot was the mistake of being very judgmental."

He simply nodded. "Of course."

She looked a bit irritated. "Why do you say 'of course'?"

"Remember," said Dr. Scott, "I am always thinking in terms of The 50-50 Rule."

"Right. And so. . ."

"And so what was Joe's second mistake?" Dr. Scott asked.

"To always assume he was being attacked–to play that game you call Victim," she responded.

"Exactly. And what are the odds that a man who tends to play Victim—who always assumes he is going to be attacked–would marry a woman who was frequently judgmental–an Attacker?"

Elizabeth brightened. "It's the compulsive talker man and the compulsive listener woman!"

"Right. The one who plays Victim marries the one who plays Attacker, which allows each of them to stay in their comfort zone."

She looked ill at ease. "My comfort zone was to be an Attacker?"

"Sure–what better way to avoid being IT?"

"So I married a man who would expect me to make him IT."

Dr. Scott nodded. "Which you then proceeded to do."

Elizabeth shook her head. "That's awful."

"Remember, it's not helpful to judge the pattern," he cautioned. "It's only important to see it clearly, so that you can decide to do it differently."

Elizabeth declared, "I WILL do it differently."

Dr. Scott nodded sympathetically. "I believe you will. But I'm not the one who needs to hear that."

Elizabeth turned to Joe. "I will begin to break that pattern starting right now. You are way too precious to attack and I just can't keep doing that any longer."

Joe struggled to make eye contact. "That has been a really painful part of our marriage. Too painful for me to talk about right now. But thank you."

She gently placed her hand on top of his. "I love you."

Joe kept his head down but nodded. "Me too."

After a long pause, Dr. Scott said, "I'm guessing you can pretty much figure out your next homework assignment."

Joe smiled and said, "We are to take the individual parts that we each contribute to our patterns and see how they fit together, so we will see our mutual patterns clearly."

"Right," confirmed Dr. Scott. "Then next time I can teach you how you can break those patterns every time."

"That would be a huge breakthrough," replied Joe, enthusiastically.

"Yes, it will be," corrected Dr. Scott.

"Okay," Joe grinned, "that <u>will</u> be a huge breakthrough."

"Right."

Elizabeth hesitated. "I don't know exactly how to say this. I don't want our homework conversation about our dysfunctions to turn into a family-bashing conversation where we just blame our parents for our troubles."

Dr. Scott responded, "I'm glad, since they're not to blame."

Elizabeth persisted. "But didn't you say that we learned our dysfunctions in our families?"

"You did learn them there. But your family members are not the ones who keep those patterns alive today. You are. And you are the ones who can change those patterns, starting today. Just as it would be wrong to condemn yourself, it would be wrong to spend another moment condemning your families."

"We just need to learn the lesson," she replied.

Dr. Scott nodded. "Right. See the mistakes clearly, learn the lesson, and ask God to transform your thinking, starting today."

"Got it."

"I'll see the two of you next week."

SUMMARY OF CHAPTER 5

- Getting healthier doesn't mean you will no longer re-visit your old patterns. It means you will catch those patterns sooner and sooner and will recover from them more and more quickly.
- Any two people who are willing to learn the simple rules of constructive communication can create a powerful relationship. In fact, we were created by God to do exactly that.
- Soon others will be asking you how you were able to create such a loving relationship and you will be teaching those others how to live in right relationship. This is the most effective possible form of evangelism.
- Although the mistakes you make don't matter, learning from those mistakes matters terribly. Patrick Carnes, one of the leading writers in the field of sexual addictions, says, "Addictive people don't make any more mistakes than the average person–that's not the problem. The problem is that they keep making the same mistakes over and over again."
- Healthy people actually make even more mistakes than TAG-playing people because they don't quit when they start making them.
- TAG players sacrifice any chance at happiness, right relationship, and fulfillment, just to avoid being wrong.
- The discussion of the homework assignment will require: being proud of the effort, focusing on what you did right, and the willingness to learn life's lessons without judgment.
- We can be sure we are playing the game called Rehearsal whenever we see ourselves preparing a response at a time when we are supposed to

be listening. We are especially likely to play this game in the presence of an Attacker.

- We experience freedom in Christ the instant we admit our mistakes openly and without qualifiers and realize that we are the beloved, just the same.

- As soon as we quit playing TAG, our "need" to protect ourselves is replaced with compassion for others.

- This compassion triggers a powerful desire to change our previously hurtful behaviors.

- Victim is a game we play when we start with the assumption that we are going to be IT.

- If we move into the Fixer role, before taking the time to truly understand, we undermine people's self-confidence, offer useless suggestions, and allow TAG to begin.

- We each contribute to our TAG-playing patterns and to the way in which we set up our future patterns.

- Our part of the pattern is based on certain lies that we have consistently told ourselves.

- The pattern will change only when we replace those lies with the truth–about who we are (precious beyond the telling) and about what we really want (intimate connections).

- An Attacker uses criticism of others as a way to avoid being IT themselves. We call this interaction pattern Constant TAG.

- As the 50-50 Rule would suggest that Attackers ("everything is all your fault") will frequently marry Victims ("you're right—everything really

IS all my fault") and Controllers or Fixers ("do it my way because your way is stupid") will frequently marry people who play Rehearsal ("let me explain why my idea isn't stupid").

EXERCISE #4

Now that you each understand your part of the dysfunctional pattern(s) you get into, put the pieces together in a way that allows you to see the whole picture–the way in which each step of the pattern sets up the next step. Remember, no one is IT, including you. This is just an exercise designed to heighten your mutual understanding of the pattern, so that the next chapter will make even more sense to you.

In the space provided, please sketch out the interaction as accurately as you can.

	I Said (and felt)	They Said (and felt)
1.)		
2.)		
3.)		
4.)		

	I Said (and felt)	They Said (and felt)
5.)		
6.)		
7.)		
8.)		

CHAPTER 6:

Breaking the Patterns

"Welcome back. Are you both ready to get started?"

Joe smiled in anticipation. "Doctor, we have been eagerly awaiting today's session because we really want to learn how to break our TAG patterns."

"Great. Let's get right into it. Show me the chart you made of an existing pattern."

Joe started by explaining, "We decided to analyze the argument that triggered our coming to you—a dumb argument we had about the mail one morning, just as I was about to leave for work. Here's how it went, as best as we can recall. We wrote down what we said and then the roles we thought we each were playing."

Joe	Elizabeth
"Honey, I can't find this week's bills." (whiny tone)	
[assumes Victim role, implies Elizabeth is IT]	

Joe	Elizabeth
	"You're the grouch who demanded that the bills not be put on his desk." (harsh tone)
	[Attacker, calls Joe names to make him IT; "You language"]
"All I ever said was I needed my desk to be less cluttered. I never said that we shouldn't put the mail there." (defensive tone, seeking approval)	
[we saw how defending IS playing TAG]	
	"You should have organized things yesterday, when you had the time." (criticism instead of approval)
	[Fixer, message = Joe is hopeless and IT]
"You know that I have been really busy lately. And besides, I can't do it without help."	
[Rehearsal–"why you are IT"]	
	"I'm not the one who brings in the mail anyway. You know that." (critical; implies that Joe is stupid)
	[Attack mode–Joe is still IT]
"Did Sabrina bring it in?" (placating)	
[Victim, asks to be let off the hook]	
	"Sabrina always brings it in." (sharp tone)
	[pure Attacker; no dice]

Joe	Elizabeth
"Why are you so upset with me? I didn't do anything wrong." ("poor me" tone) [pure Victim, plus Rehearsal]	
	"I'm not upset. I just don't like getting blamed for things that aren't my fault." (feels scared but sounds angry) [Attacker–"you did it wrong" = "you're IT"]
"I wasn't blaming you–I was just asking where the bills were so we wouldn't lose them. You know, we did almost lose one last week." (defensive) [Rehearsal and implied shifting of blame]	
	"I've never lost a bill in my life." (self-righteous) ["I'm not IT and you're bad for implying so" = IT]
"Well, we easily could if we don't come up with a better system." (fearful) [Victim and Rehearsal]	
	"I don't want to talk about this anymore. Have a good day at work." (self-righteous anger) [Fixer, exerts control by ending the conversation]

Dr. Scott was clearly impressed. "Wow, the two of you did your homework assignment very well; you were very thorough and very honest."

Joe smiled, accepting the compliment. "Thanks. It was actually pretty easy, once we got rolling."

"Did you have any problems at all while doing the homework?" asked Dr. Scott.

Joe shook his head. "It was hard to get started, in part because we expected it to be an ugly conversation. But it was actually fun, in a way."

Elizabeth agreed. "Yes, we kept making excuses at first, but then, after supper three nights ago, Joe put his foot down and said we needed to get started. I knew he was right, so I went along."

"But honey, you did a lot more than just go along."

She nodded, happily. "Yes, once I got into it and really started to see how our patterns played out, it became like a game–a scientific mystery that we were going to solve. Like Joe said, it was actually fun once we got past our fear."

"How long did it take the two of you once you got started?" asked Dr. Scott.

Joe responded. "We actually had several conversations about it. We talked for about 30 minutes that first night. Then after that we chatted a couple more different times, as new ideas occurred to us. The chart we showed you is the result of having continually fine-tuned our original ideas."

Elizabeth nodded. "It was fun to use our analytical minds, to bounce our ideas off each another, and to keep getting more and more clear about the pattern."

Dr. Scott replied, "The process the two of you just described illustrates two concepts that I love to talk to couples about."

"Okay, I'll be the set-up girl–what two concepts?"

Dr. Scott smiled and continued. "First, that a good marriage is best understood as an ongoing conversation."

"That's a neat idea," she replied, clearly intrigued.

"Thanks. By that I mean that in a great relationship, a decision is not a one-time event but a process in which two connected people continue to lovingly interact until they reach the point of clarity. That's exactly what the two of you did."

"So we got it right!" Elizabeth exclaimed.

"You did it great," said Dr. Scott, enjoying her excitement.

Joe smiled. "You're right, doctor. The on-going nature of the conversation was extremely helpful. What was the second concept you mentioned?"

Dr. Scott explained, "In the game of TAG, the goal of any conversation is to not be wrong ourselves. In healthy relationships, however, the goal of any conversation is to understand the other person. Once we are clear about that goal, we can have enjoyable conversations about even the most difficult of topics."

"No more arguments, ever?" asked Joe.

"Right—not as long as you are clear about your goal," agreed Dr. Scott.

"Wow." Joe looked thoughtful.

Elizabeth remained unconvinced. "But everyone says that arguments are a natural part of marriage."

"Oh, they occur in every marriage, I am sure of that," replied Dr. Scott. "But what you will come to understand is that they are literally a waste of your time."

"Always?" she asked skeptically.

"Always," Dr. Scott affirmed. "Think about it. Since the goal of any real conversation is to understand the other person, what do we need to do, mostly?"

"Listen?" Elizabeth guessed.

"Exactly. And what is the one thing no one is doing during an argument?"

Elizabeth smiled. "I get it. No one is listening. So it can never be a real conversation."

Dr. Scott nodded his head vigorously. "Right. So it's a total waste of time."

"Then how do you have a real conversation?" she wondered.

"That's a good question and it leads us right to the point where Joe started us off this week–breaking the TAG-playing patterns the two of you get into. As soon as you break those patterns, you can start having real meaningful conversations about any topic."

"Great–where do we start?" asked Elizabeth enthusiastically.

Dr. Scott began, "There are two things you need to understand in order to stop the game of TAG forever: In TAG no one ever tells the truth and no one ever hears the truth. I will start with the first one–the one where no one ever tells the truth."

Joe looked puzzled. "Are you saying that we're liars?"

Dr. Scott shook his head. "No, just that when you play TAG you avoid telling the actual truth when you talk."

Joe was clearly confused. "I don't get it. I thought the problem in TAG was that people were TOO willing to tell the truth."

"No," corrected Dr. Scott. "In TAG-paying families, no one ever tells the truth. A lot of mean words might be spoken (or unspoken), but the truth is never actually said."

Elizabeth wrinkled her brow and asked, "How can you say that?"

Dr. Scott replied, "Because in TAG everything that gets said is hurtful and the truth is never hurtful."

"Doesn't the truth sometimes hurt?" she persisted.

Dr. Scott shook his head. "No, never, because the only things I know for sure are things about myself–the things I think, feel, or want. So if I am telling you the truth I am only telling you about myself; every sentence will start with 'I.' In TAG, on the other hand, what does every sentence start with?"

Elizabeth understood. "Just like in our pattern, everything starts with 'you,' doesn't it?"

"Exactly," Dr. Scott affirmed. "In TAG, every statement starts with 'you'–there is a lot of what I call 'you language,' as in 'you are always late' or 'you are the bad one' or 'you will never learn.' Those statements can't be my truth because they're not about me."

Elizabeth persisted, saying, "So in a real conversation, you don't ever talk about the other person?"

"No–you just share information about yourself. That's what we mean by intimacy. In an intimate conversation, each of us is saying, 'this is who I am,' while the other person listens intently."

Joe concluded, "In a real conversation, an intimate conversation, there literally can't be any attacks, since you are only talking about yourself."

Dr. Scott nodded at his two prize pupils. "Right, that's the beauty of it. Now in order to have an intimate conversation and not get pulled into TAG, you will need to be clear about two things. First, as I have indicated, when you are the speaker you need to use 'I language,' not 'you language.' You need to make it explicitly clear that you are sharing information about yourself, not attacking the other person."

Joe was excited. "Can we practice while we are still with you?"

Dr. Scott was agreeable. "Yes, in fact, I was going to suggest that. Joe, would you like to start?"

"Sure. There's something I really need to talk to Elizabeth about and this would be a great place to learn how to do it correctly."

Elizabeth smiled and said, "Should I be nervous?"

Joe shook his head. "No, I don't want to be attacking in any way. It's just that I don't like the way that you discipline the kids."

Dr. Scott interrupted. "Joe, in that sentence you did not tell us anything about yourself. What are your own thoughts and feelings regarding discipline?"

Joe looked confused. "I'm not sure what you mean."

Dr. Scott paused. "Well, let's start here. What happens when you try to discipline the kids?"

Joe replied, "They ask me for something they know is against our rules. If I say 'no,' they go to their mom. She gives in and off they go. That's the problem–there's no discipline."

Dr. Scott, seeking to clarify Joe's thinking, said, "I'm thinking that if you were to put that into 'I language,' you might say something like, 'Whenever there is a need for discipline, I end up feeling all alone—abandoned. Plus, I want our kids to have happy, productive lives and I worry that if they don't learn to follow appropriate rules their lives will go poorly.' Is that a fair summary?"

Joe smiled. "You're good at this. That was almost perfect. The only thing I would add is that I am starting to see how fun it is to do things with Elizabeth, instead of against her, and I would like to have that 'me and you' feeling when we're dealing with the kids."

Dr. Scott turned to Elizabeth and asked, "Elizabeth, did all of that make sense to you?"

"It made perfect sense," she replied. "In fact, everything Joe wants, I would want for him."

Dr. Scott nodded and said, "Right–as soon as we begin to tell the truth, instead of playing TAG, we find that we are in perfect alignment with each another. Instead of falsely believing that we are on opposite sides, we see the truth–that we are compassionately connected through God's love and that everything the other person wants, we would want for them."

A light bulb went on for Elizabeth. "That's why in an intimate conversation there are no arguments!"

"Right," confirmed Dr. Scott. "There WILL be interesting discussions as to how we might best achieve our mutual objectives but there will be no arguments as to what those objectives should be or as to our desire to achieve those objectives as a team."

"Thank you. That's very helpful," replied an appreciative Elizabeth.

"Great. Let's hear your 'I language' response to Joe's statements."

She took a deep breath and said, "Okay, here goes. I want us to be a team too. I don't actually like giving in to the kids. I used to tell myself I just wanted them to like me but now I realize I was just trying not to be the bad one–I was trying to avoid being IT."

Dr. Scott said, proudly, "Good for you. Anything else?"

Elizabeth hesitated, then replied, "Well, I do sometimes think that Joe is too hard on the kids."

"Do you want to translate that into 'I language'?"

"I thought I had."

"Nope. Who was the subject of that sentence?"

"Joe was."

Dr. Scott nodded. "Right. Want to tell us about yourself?"

She tried again. "How about this? I want the kids to develop a strong relationship with Joe and to see him as the good man that he is, but I'm worried that if all they hear from him is the negative stuff they will tune him out, drift away, and never get a chance to really bond with him."

"Very impressive. Joe, my guess is that you are in total agreement with everything you just heard."

"Well, sure. I want a good relationship with the kids and I have been worried about all of those same things."

Dr. Scott responded, "I thought so. Now all the two of you have to do is decide how you are going to work as a team to achieve your mutual objectives. It's a good example of what I always say–in great relationships, the conversations are never about 'if,' they're always about 'how.' "

Elizabeth smiled. "This is fun. Can we do another one?"

"Go ahead."

"I was always telling Joe that he should spend less money and quit buying certain types of things. I see now that not only was I playing my usual Fixer role, I also was using 'you language,' which left him feeling attacked and led to us having 'if conversations' instead of 'how conversations.' "

Joe nodded his agreement and waited for Elizabeth to finish.

Elizabeth plunged ahead. "So here is my new 'I language' attempt to address that topic more constructively. Joe, I would really like for us to be able to travel more and to work less. And I'm afraid if we don't start making smarter financial decisions, we will never get to that point."

Joe looked surprised. "I had no idea–I just thought you were being controlling."

She shook her head. "Our most fun-filled times have come when we have been on vacation and I want our life together to start feeling more like a vacation."

Joe grinned. "I'm all for that!"

Dr. Scott concluded by saying, "Good work, you guys. I can see you are ready to learn the second step in breaking the TAG cycle."

"What is the second step?" Joe wondered.

"Remember when I said that in TAG no one ever tells the truth? Well, in TAG, no one ever hears the truth either."

"What do you mean by that?" he asked.

Dr. Scott continued. "Well, if you are having a real conversation with someone and they are talking, who are they talking about?"

"Themselves," Joe responded correctly.

"Right. But in TAG, we always react defensively—as if they were talking about us. That's what I mean when I say that no one ever hears the truth."

Joe thought for a moment and said, "So whenever I get defensive, that's a sign I'm not hearing the truth."

"Right," affirmed Dr. Scott. "You are hearing some distorted version of the truth, in which you take everything that is said, turn it around, and act as if it is about you."

"How can Elizabeth and I break that pattern?"

Dr. Scott responded, "Here's how I think of it. When I am the listener, I need to keep my ego out of the conversation."

Joe shook his head and said, "You lost me on that last part, Dr. Scott."

Dr. Scott elaborated. "If my wife, Rose, says to me, 'That sarcastic comment you made about my brother is the kind of thing that hurts my feelings,' I could allow my ego to get in the way and I could start thinking that her comment was a statement about me. Then I probably would get defensive and start playing TAG."

Joe persisted. "How can that statement not be about you?"

"Think about it," replied Dr. Scott. "It's not about me at all. It's completely about Rose–she's just telling me that a particular type of comment is hurtful to her. As her husband, that's a helpful piece of information to have, don't you think?"

Joe agreed. "Yes, when you think about it that way."

"If my mind was clear, I would respond by saying, 'Thanks honey. It's helpful to know that about YOU. That helps me to understand YOU better. I will bear that in mind in the future, when I am talking to YOU.' Do you see what I mean?"

Joe sat up straight and said, "That might be the single most liberating thing you have ever said to me."

"I'm glad. Just remember, as the listener, keep your ego out of it. The other person is simply giving you helpful information about themselves."

Elizabeth said simply, "That's why the truth is never hurtful. Because it's only information and it's not even information about you–it's just helpful information about the other person."

Dr. Scott nodded. "Right. And here's the really cool part. When I drop the TAG response and understand that Rose is simply sharing with me some helpful information about herself, we start to have far more interesting discussions."

"What do you mean?" she asked.

Dr. Scott continued. "Well, if Rose tells me that certain remarks about her brother hurt her feelings and I understand that she is just sharing information about herself, it frees me from responding defensively ('I was only kidding,' 'You shouldn't take my remarks so personally,' 'How was I to know?') and allows me to ask questions, instead. Like I might ask, 'How come, honey?' or something creative like that."

"That would be a different conversation," Elizabeth agreed.

Dr. Scott nodded. "And a more interesting one, I promise you. I might find out that she was mean to her brother when she was younger and she feels really badly about that now. I might find out that her brother was really protective of her while she was growing up and that she feels very loyal to him now because of that. I literally don't know what I will find out but I do know that our conversation will be a lot more interesting than it would be if we had played TAG."

Joe agreed too. "That would be a far more interesting conversation, for sure. And let's face it, any real conversation would be infinitely more interesting than hearing myself get all defensive again, in the same old way I always used to."

Elizabeth chimed in. "This whole way of having a conversation is so cool. I really want to get good at this."

Dr. Scott replied, "Great–let's start right now. Which of you would like to share something about yourself?"

Joe said, "Let's go back to the ugly conversation we outlined at the beginning of the session so that we can learn how to do that differently."

"Okay."

"I started off by asking Elizabeth why the bills weren't in their usual place. As we already noted, that was just a way for me to make her IT. I understand that now."

Dr. Scott said, "I'm glad you're clear about that now. If you had started the conversation by telling the truth, which is always about yourself, instead of playing TAG, which is always about her, what might you have said?"

Joe considered the question, then replied, "I might have just said, 'Honey, I'm a little worried because I can't find the bills,' or something simple like that."

"Perfect," beamed Dr. Scott. "Way to tell the truth. And Elizabeth, if you were clear that Joe's comment was just a way of sharing information about himself, how might you respond to such a comment?"

"My knee-jerk reaction, of course, would be to start with the assumption that I was being attacked and that it was my fault he couldn't find the bills. But now I get it–that would be an example of letting my ego get in the way, as you say."

"So how might you do it differently?" asked Dr. Scott.

"Well, since it's just a piece of information about him and he's feeling nervous, I could try to reassure him. Or I could ask where he had looked so far and then help him."

"Beautiful. Let's talk about reassurance for a moment. What do you guys find reassuring?"

"What do you mean?" she asked.

Dr. Scott tried again. "What do you find comforting?"

Elizabeth replied, "Gentle touch and kind words, I suppose."

"Like what?"

"Well, in this case, I might put my hand on Joe's arm and tell him that it would be okay and that we could look for the bills together after the kids left for school."

"Joe, would you find that reassuring?"

"Absolutely. Touch has always been our best way of connecting and I would appreciate the help, too, I'm sure."

Dr. Scott responded, "Okay, great. I want to stop the tape, so to speak, for just a minute and talk about reassurance. Then we can go back and pick up the rest of that old conversation. Is that all right?"

Both Joe and Elizabeth nodded their heads.

Dr. Scott began by saying, "Here is why reassurance is so important. Remember how I told you that in TAG everyone felt alone and that there was only one emotion and it wasn't anger?"

Elizabeth thoughtfully said, "Right–you said that the game was always about fear."

Dr. Scott nodded. "And when we're afraid, what do we need?"

"Reassurance?" she guessed.

"Exactly. When my daughter wakes up in the middle of the night and is afraid that there is a monster in her closet, what does she need me to do?"

Elizabeth smiled a mother's smile and said, "To put your arm around her, tell her that you are there with her, and let her know that everything will be okay."

"In other words," replied Dr. Scott, "I would need to use touch and words to let her know she was not alone and she therefore didn't need to be afraid. Right?"

"Right," she agreed.

"Before we could possibly have a rational conversation about the fact that the 'monster' was just the teddy bear in her closet, she would first need to feel connected to me–to quit feeling afraid."

Joe interjected, a bit impatiently, "That's all true, Dr. Scott, but how does that relate to us?"

Dr. Scott explained further. "Well, since TAG is all about fear, reassurance–the alleviation of fear–is a great way to break the cycle. And once I understand that the things you say are all about you, it frees me up from being defensive and triggers compassion . . ."

"The cork popping back up!" Joe exclaimed.

Dr. Scott smiled broadly. "Precisely! And once I feel compassion for a person who is scared, my natural reaction is to comfort them, which is great, because that's exactly what they need."

Joe nodded, conclusively. "I get it. Once they feel comforted and no longer afraid, then you can have a rational conversation with them. Like Elizabeth helping me to figure out where the bills are, once I'm no longer anxious."

"Right. That's why I wanted to know what was comforting to each of you. It's an important thing to know about each other because it's what each of us needs when we feel scared. And the people who play TAG are indeed scared, even though they tend to act like they're mad."

"What are the most common ways to comfort each other?" Elizabeth wondered.

"The four ways that are almost always helpful are: non-invasive touch, empathy, the word 'we,' and offers to help," explained Dr. Scott. "All of them help us to feel as if we're not alone, which is what we need in order to get past our fear."

Elizabeth asked, "Could you give me examples of each one?"

"Actually, the example you gave came close to combining all four of them. If Joe comes to you, says that he's scared about the bills, and you put your hand on his arm, and say, 'I can see how that would make you nervous. I would be glad to help you look as soon as the kids go to school–I'm sure we'll find them if we look together,' you would have accomplished all four."

Elizabeth joked, "So I'm just naturally brilliant?"

Dr. Scott smiled. "Yes, but don't get a swelled head. We all are. Loving reassurance is what we all do naturally as we quit playing TAG and get our egos out of the way long enough to hear the truth."

"Now can we go back the homework assignment now and finish doing that old conversation differently?"

"Sure, Joe," replied Dr. Scott. "Let's pick up where we left off. What happened next?"

"After Elizabeth made me IT by saying, 'I'm not the grouch who insisted that the bills not be put on his desk.' I got all defensive and said something like 'All I said was I needed my desk to be less cluttered.' "

"If instead of getting defensive, you had heard the truth, what would you have heard and how might you have responded with compassion?"

"I would have heard my honey saying that she felt attacked for a problem that I had created. And I could have reassured her by using gentle touch and telling her that it wasn't her fault—that she wasn't IT."

"Great," responded Dr. Scott. "In my family, we have a saying, 'Honey, you're not the bad one,' which is our way of letting the other person know that they're not IT."

Joe nodded in approval. "I like that. It's simple and to the point."

"Yes, and it breaks the cycle immediately."

Joe asked, "What do you say when you feel attacked–like the other person is trying to make you be IT?"

"Remember, to break TAG when we are speaking we have to tell the truth, which always will involve using 'I language' and trying to speak only about ourselves. So we say, 'I feel like the bad one,' which is a way to convey the necessary information without attacking the other person–without saying 'you're making me be IT,' which is just a way to play TAG about playing TAG."

"That's so simple," Joe noted, with a note of disbelief.

"Yes, the right way is always simple."

Elizabeth hesitated and then asked, "But does it work in real life?"

Dr. Scott replied, with great conviction, "In fact, it's the only way that does work. Everything else is just a way to play TAG, which never works."

Joe said, "So, when you're talking you just speak <u>your</u> truth, using 'I language,' and when you're listening you just ask simple questions and listen for <u>their</u> truth, which will always lead to a compassionate response which will calm their fears."

"Right–and to an interesting conversation."

"I think I get it," Joe replied.

"I think I understand too," Elizabeth said. "I can see, though, that the most difficult part for me will be to keep my ego out of it while I am listening."

Dr. Scott gave a sympathetic nod. "I think that's the hardest part for a lot of people. Here's what I do to help myself with that. Who does a little child think that everything is about?"

Elizabeth grinned. "Themselves, of course. For a little child, everything is about me."

"Right," affirmed Dr. Scott. "So when I begin to feel defensive, I tell myself, 'yah, yah, Richard, it's all about you. What are you, three years old?' And by teasing myself, it breaks the spell and I come back to reality—the reality that the other person is simply telling me something about themselves."

"Okay, I'll remember that if I feel myself starting to get defensive," she promised.

"Great. Your homework assignment is to take that old conversation and ask yourselves, at each step of the way, 'How could I have broken the pattern by speaking my actual truth if I were the speaker and by hearing the truth if I were the listener?'"

Joe asked, "So, we each do that, for each step of the interaction?"

Dr. Scott nodded and said, "Yes, and when it's your turn to speak the truth, please remember this. In TAG, no one speaks the truth, on either a verbal or an emotional level."

"What do you mean?" Joe wondered, clearly confused.

Dr. Scott explained, saying, "In TAG, the language used is always in 'you' form, and the supposed emotion is always some variation of anger. In reality, however, the truth is always in 'I' form and our emotion is rarely that of anger. We are far more likely to be feeling anxious, fearful, disappointed, let down, abandoned, sad, confused, or frustrated than we are to feel angry. So when you are practicing telling your truth, tell the whole truth–a truth which will always be about you and will almost never be about anger."

Elizabeth wondered, "How can we tell if we really are angry or if that's just a cover up for whatever we're actually feeling?"

Dr. Scott explained by saying, "My pathetically simplistic Two-Emotion Theory of Life is this–'we get mad about stuff that happens to us and sad about stuff that doesn't.' Does that make sense?"

"Not yet," she smiled, waiting for clarification.

Dr. Scott continued. "I was talking to a young man a few years ago who said, 'My dad was abusive to me while I was growing up and I'm still SO mad about that.' I said, 'I believe you're still somewhat mad about the times he yelled at you and the two times he even hit you. But I also believe you are far more sad about all of the things that didn't occur–about all of your ballgames he didn't attend, all of the reassuring talks the two of you didn't have, all of the father-son activities that didn't take place, and all of the promises that didn't materialize.' The young man started crying right in my office."

Elizabeth checked her understanding. "I think I understand. We get mad about the things that are actively hurtful to us and sad about things that we wanted to happen that didn't happen."

"Right," replied Dr. Scott. "That's why it can be difficult at times to know why we are sad–because we literally are sad about something that never occurred!"

"And you think that we are actually sad a lot more often than we are mad?" she asked.

"Yes, especially in a really important relationship like a marriage or a deep friendship. We have so many hopes and dreams for those relationships that it is easy for us to feel let down, disappointed, or discouraged–all of the emotions that are related to sadness."

Elizabeth was puzzled. "So why do we pretend to be mad instead?"

Dr. Scott explained. "Partly because it's harder to identify what we are sad about, and partly because anger makes us feel big and powerful, whereas sadness makes us feel small and vulnerable."

Elizabeth nodded. "That's why, in non-TAG relationships, there is so much reassurance being given–it's because we willingly make ourselves so much more vulnerable."

Dr. Scott nodded. "Precisely. In intimate relationships, where the TAG playing is kept to a minimum, the speakers are free to tell the truth, which is more often about sad than it is about mad. And the listeners are free to respond to that vulnerability with empathy and compassion–with words and touch that can heal those hurts."

Elizabeth said, with both joy and wistfulness, "That sounds very loving."

Dr. Scott replied, "That's exactly what every God-led relationship is. Do the two of you feel ready to go and do your homework assignment?"

Joe smiled. "I think I speak for both of us when I say that we are anxious and excited about this assignment."

Elizabeth nodded her agreement.

"Okay, good. Remember, we're not looking for perfection. Just an honest attempt to tell the truth and to hear the truth in love. I'll see you next week."

SUMMARY OF CHAPTER 6

- It is important to look at our patterns objectively–like a pair of scientists who are seeking to understand one of the mysteries of life. That way we can learn the necessary lessons, instead of playing TAG.
- A marriage is best understood as an on-going conversation.
- Arguments are not an example of such a conversation. Arguments are literally a waste of time because no one is listening.
- The truth is never hurtful because my truth is always about me, not about you.
- In TAG, no one ever tells the truth or hears the truth.
- To break that cycle, we need to speak our truth ("I language") when we are talking and we need to keep our ego out of things when we are listening. All "you language" is a sign we are not speaking the truth and all defensiveness is a sign we are not hearing the truth.
- When we speak honestly, we share important information about ourselves.
- When we listen non-defensively, we ask questions about them, instead of making statements about ourselves. This is the beginning point for all interesting conversations.
- When we speak the truth, we must speak both the factual and emotional truth, which requires that we know the difference between sad and mad.
- We get mad about what happens to us and sad about what doesn't.
- Many people act mad, even when they are actually sad or scared, because it can be difficult to know why we are sad (since our sadness is

about an event that did not occur) and because it feels less vulnerable to be mad.

- When we understand that our partner is not talking about us and is mostly sad or scared, it frees us to comfort them, instead of defending ourselves.

- The four most common forms of reassurance are non-invasive touch (a hand on their shoulder), empathy ("I understand"), the word "we" ("we can figure this out together," and offers to help ("where should we start?").

- When we are starting to feel like we are IT, we can break the cycle by making a simple "I language" statement like "I'm starting to feel like I'm IT."

- If our partner is starting to sound defensive, we can break the cycle by simply saying, "Honey, you're not IT," or "Honey, you're not the bad one."

EXERCISE #5

Go back to your old patterns, look at each step in those patterns, and ask yourself:

1.) If I had told my (verbal and emotional) truth at each step along the way, what would I have said at each of those steps?

2.) If I had heard the truth, instead of getting defensive, what would I have heard?

3.) How might I have responded in a more compassionate or reassuring way?

4) What sorts of responses do I personally find to be most reassuring?

CHAPTER 7:

Variations of the Game

"Well, how did your homework assignment go?"

Joe grinned. "It sure helped us to discover that we aren't good at telling the truth or hearing the truth."

Elizabeth agreed. "We actually had fun doing that old conversation differently; that was very constructive. We agreed that every argument does start with someone either not telling or not hearing it."

Dr. Scott was impressed. "Wow, that's really cool. I'm proud of you. Then why did Joe say you two were so bad at it?"

"Because whenever we tried to implement it in real life, we caught ourselves going back into our old patterns," she explained.

"But you did eventually notice that you were doing it?" asked Dr. Scott.

"Yes, eventually," Elizabeth confirmed.

"Super," he replied.

"Really?" she asked.

"Sure. Didn't I ever tell you about the make-believe story a friend of mine always tells—the story about the open manhole?"

Elizabeth looked uncertain. "I don't think so."

Dr. Scott elaborated. "My friend tells this story of a guy who was walking down the street on his way to work one day. There was a manhole in the street that was missing its cover and not realizing it, he fell in. The next day he remembered it but only at the last minute and he fell in again. The next day he remembered it at the very last second and almost fell in but was able to save himself. Then the next day he remembered in plenty of time and the day after that he took a different way to work."

With a straight face, Elizabeth asked, "Your friend likes to tell this story?"

Dr. Scott smiled. "Well, I admit he is kind of twisted, but I believe the story does indeed have a point."

"I know, I was just teasing you," she reassured him. "And I get the point, I think. When we are breaking a destructive cycle, we don't break it instantaneously. Like you said before, we break it by catching ourselves sooner and sooner in the cycle."

Dr. Scott nodded and smiled. "Perfectly said. And so, since the two of you are indeed starting to catch yourselves, albeit rather late in the cycle, I know eventually you will eliminate most of those interactions altogether."

"How soon is eventually?" she wondered.

"You know how the process works. There are only three ways to get better at anything."

Joe smiled. "Practice, practice, and more practice."

"Right. If you practice diligently over the next two weeks, you will already be able to tell that you are getting significantly better at interrupting the old patterns and replacing them with truly interesting conversations. Two weeks after that, you will be even better at it."

"Why did you say 'two weeks' when we meet with you every week?" Joe asked.

"Because I think we can start tapering our sessions at this point," replied Dr. Scott. "And because I will be leading a seminar next week that could help you to understand the game of TAG at a whole new level and how to break through the game in simple, yet powerful ways. I think it is perfectly suited to where the two of you are in the process and would be the fastest way for you to get you to the next level if you attended the seminar."

"I would love to learn even more about TAG!" Elizabeth exclaimed.

Joe, in his more factual way, asked, "Dr. Scott, what exactly is the seminar about?"

"It's about breaking four of the most common TAG patterns, not just in the marriage but in other relationships as well."

Joe was agreeable. "That does sound helpful. Now that we know what we know, we see people playing TAG all around us–at home, at work, even at church."

"Yes, it happens everywhere and it has the same destructive effect on all other relationships that it has on marriages–it destroys them. It's like an acid that eats away at them from the inside out," lamented Dr. Scott.

"That's a powerful image," commented Elizabeth. "And it's an accurate one too. You think that you are doing fine and that the two of you have a relationship that is okay. But over time TAG kills it, one small step at a time, so gradually you hardly notice it. Then one day you realize the two of you have 'a communication problem' and can hardly stand to be in each other's presence."

Dr. Scott was truly amazed. "You really do have an awesome way with words."

Elizabeth blushed. "Thanks."

"Joe, before I describe the seminar, I would like to hear more about the homework assignment and about each of your efforts to tell and hear the truth. Is that okay?"

"That's fine with me, doctor. I have learned to trust the way you lead this process."

Dr. Scott smiled. "High praise indeed–thanks."

Joe simply nodded.

Dr. Scott inquired, "What did each of you find to be the hardest part of breaking the cycle?"

Elizabeth said, "I expected to struggle with hearing the truth. But I discovered it was actually much harder for me to tell the truth."

"That makes perfect sense to me," replied Dr. Scott.

"Why is that?" she wondered.

Dr. Scott elaborated. "Well, your contributions to the old patterns were generally about giving unsolicited advice and about being controlling. In short, you tended to tell other people what to do and how to feel. Right?"

Elizabeth flinched. "Yes, although you make it sound pretty bad."

Dr. Scott reminded her, "Please don't judge it. It just was what it was."

She straightened up. "Okay, yes, my 50% of the problem tended to involve telling others what to do instead of letting them be on my team."

Dr. Scott continued. "Since your contribution tended to involve a lot of 'you language,' it just makes sense to me that for you the hardest part of making the change would involve switching to 'I language'–to telling the truth, from your own perspective."

"That makes sense," she acknowledged. "Could you please help me to believe that my being controlling doesn't make me a bad person?"

"Sure," agreed Dr. Scott. "What emotion always drives TAG?"

"Fear," she responded.

"Right," confirmed Dr. Scott. "And you were afraid people would do the wrong thing, afraid that people would think badly of you or your husband, afraid to let anyone be on your team."

"True," she acknowledged.

"And what's the fastest way to help a person to get over their fear?" asked Dr. Scott.

"Reassurance."

"So what kind of reassurance would you like to receive from Joe?"

She turned toward her husband and said in a small, quiet voice, "I would like you to hold me and tell me that you understand–you understand that I was scared and I didn't know what else to do."

Joe put both of his arms around her and spoke gently, "I love you, honey. I know you were just scared, mostly because you felt as though you were all alone. From now on, we'll deal with everything together."

After a bit, the two of them straightened up and Elizabeth said to Dr. Scott, "I'm sorry about that."

Dr. Scott responded in a very strict tone of voice. "Please don't ever say that to me again. I mean it. Not ever."

Elizabeth looked startled. "What did I do wrong?"

Dr. Scott explained, "You apologized for the purest, most perfectly godly thing you've ever done. I want you to celebrate what just happened, not apologize for it."

"What exactly did I do?" she wondered.

"You asked for exactly what you wanted, with absolutely no elements of TAG, using total 'I language,' and you gave Joe the opportunity to be there for you. And then you accepted his nurturance of you. In that moment, the two of you were a perfect team," Dr. Scott pointed out.

"So you're always mean to people when they do it right?" she teased.

"No," Dr. Scott replied, "I'm strict with people when they take their absolute best self and turn it into something bad–when they play TAG against themselves. I'll talk more about that when I tell you about the seminar. In the meantime, please know that what happened between the two of you in that moment was truly worth celebrating. It was a wonderful, God-filled moment."

Joe said, "That's what I thought too. I literally loved being able to comfort you and to be there for you in that way. By talking about what <u>you</u> needed, instead of talking about <u>my</u> flaws, you made it easy for me to feel compassion and to behave in ways that I felt proud of afterwards. You helped me to be my best self."

Elizabeth smiled shyly. "Thank you, honey. I guess it's still not easy for me to be that vulnerable–to ask for what I want."

"There are only three ways . . ." began Dr. Scott.

"I know, I know, I know," interrupted Elizabeth. "Practice, practice, and more practice."

"Exactly. And you won't put in the practice if you tell yourself there is something wrong with acknowledging your real needs," Dr. Scott explained.

She nodded in understanding. "That's why you were so strict with me a minute ago."

"Right. I don't want that flawed thinking—'I shouldn't ask for what I want'—to get in the way of you becoming the woman God is calling you to be."

Elizabeth looked directly at Dr. Scott and said, "Thank you for taking such a clear stand on my behalf."

"You're welcome," he responded gently. "And just so you know, God and I will continue to fight for you. You matter to Him and you matter to me."

Joe added, "To me, too, babe. I want with my whole heart for your life to be everything that you want it to be."

"Thanks, you guys. Now can we focus on Joe for a while?"

Dr. Scott responded, "Yes, it's his turn anyway. Joe, since I know that relationships are always 50-50 and since I know Elizabeth struggled the most with telling the truth, I'm guessing that you struggled the most with hearing the truth. Is that an accurate guess?"

Joe smiled. "If I didn't know that all of your 'guesses' were actually just logical deductions, based on your having worked with thousands of couples, I would think that you had been spying on us."

Dr. Scott returned the smile. "You're right, it just makes logical sense, based both on Elizabeth's struggles this past week and on what you previously had told me were your contributions to the old patterns."

Joe was unclear. "What exactly were my contributions?"

"In our last session, you talked about playing Victim and Rehearsal," Dr. Scott reminded him. "In both of those games, the listener acts as if the speaker's words were about them, not about the speaker. So it just makes sense to me that hearing the truth might be difficult for you."

"Yes, every one of my knee-jerk reactions is based on my not hearing the truth," agreed Joe. "I constantly react as if everything is about me. I'll really need to work on teasing myself, like you said, about being childish."

"Yes," affirmed Dr. Scott, "that will help you to break the pattern because it will bring you back to reality."

"Are you saying that when I take other people's words personally, I am not thinking in reality?" Joe asked, with a challenging tone in his voice.

"Precisely."

"That makes me sound like I'm crazy!"

Dr. Scott tried to be reassuring. "No, just in a trance–it's not the same thing."

"I remember now that you talked before about being in a trance–like we've been hypnotized or something," Joe recalled.

"Right," replied Dr. Scott. "Every time you take other people's words seriously, you are not actually in the present. You are somewhere in the past, reliving an old and probably traumatic experience. You're in a reality, just not this one."

Joe looked thoughtful. "So besides reminding myself that I'm being childish, what else can I do to break that pattern?"

Dr. Scott responded, "Since you are in a trance, anything that breaks the trance will bring you back to your present reality and allow you to respond differently."

"Like what?" asked Joe.

Dr. Scott paused to collect his thoughts, then asked, "Do you remember what I always say about Think-Feel-Do?"

"Yes," said Joe, "and I frequently find that to be helpful."

"Great, then we can use that. When you are in that trance, how are you thinking about Elizabeth?"

Joe replied, "I'm thinking that I have to protect myself against her."

Dr. Scott nodded, and encouraged Joe to continue, saying, "Right, and what does that make Elizabeth?"

"She becomes the enemy," he realized.

"And who is she to you, really?" Dr. Scott prompted.

Joe looked at her and said, "She is the most precious person in my life–the woman I absolutely adore and want always to protect."

"That's exactly right," Dr. Scott replied. "So when your thinking about Elizabeth is clear–when you are back to reality–what kind of emotions does your clear thinking generate?"

Without hesitation, Joe replied, "Empathy, compassion, and the feeling of being totally in love."

"And what behaviors flow from those emotions?" asked Dr. Scott.

"Reassurance, protective reactions, and team-building behaviors."

"Right," the doctor responded. "So what is the surest way to avoid defensive listening altogether and instead behave in ways that are loving and constructive?"

"To never forget who Elizabeth is to me."

"Right. So tell her now, so you both know."

Joe turned to his wife and said, "Elizabeth, you are my soul mate–the one who I simply can't live without."

She reached out her hand for his to comfort him. "Me too."

Dr. Scott, in order to clarify his previous point, said, "Elizabeth, should Joe apologize for being so clear about his love for you?"

"No, and I understand now. When I tell her my clear truth and Joe hears my truth clearly, it's an intimate moment, a sacred moment—something to celebrate, not to regret." Dr. Scott grinned. "Congratulations, you just graduated."

"Thanks," she replied. "From what?"

"From first grade, basically."

Elizabeth frowned. "That doesn't sound too good."

"Actually, it's spectacularly important," Dr. Scott reassured her.

"Okay. What does second grade look like?" she asked.

"That's where the seminar comes in," he responded. "Now that you have the beginning tools necessary to break TAG in your marriage, it's time to learn how to do it everywhere else too."

"Does the learning process ever end?" she wondered.

"Well," Dr. Scott asked, "if a student studies extremely hard in fourth grade and does well, what is his reward?"

"He gets to go to fifth grade?" she guessed.

"Precisely."

"There is no end to this process?" she wailed.

"No," responded Dr. Scott, "there is no end. But there are huge rewards."

"And what are the rewards?" she wondered.

"The thrill of becoming even more intimately connected to God and to Joe, the excitement of learning an even more fascinating set of lessons, and the chance to begin teaching others the lessons that you have learned."

"So the process is the reward," she concluded.

"Yes," Dr. Scott agreed, "you came to see me, studied hard, did very well, and now are set to reap the rewards. And what are those rewards?"

Elizabeth gathered her thoughts for a moment, then replied, "A stronger faith life, a clearer sense of God's presence, a more powerful marriage, deeper friendships, a renewed sense of purpose, an awareness of life's possibilities, a positive impact on the lives of our children and our friends, and a chance to go to the seminar?"

"In other words, the rewards are precisely these: Everything that really matters to you is being given to you. You are being richly and joyously blessed beyond anything you can imagine by the one who, as Paul said in Ephesians 3, is able to do far more abundantly than all we ask or think."

"That's pretty cool," she said in wonder.

"It is totally cool," agreed Dr. Scott.

Joe smiled and said, "As always, I have to bring you two back to the task. Weren't we supposed to hear more about the upcoming seminar before we left?"

Dr. Scott smiled back and switched gears. "Yes, indeed you were. In the seminar, you will learn more about the four most common versions of TAG–Frozen TAG, Constant TAG, Solitaire, and Team TAG."

Joe replied, "Wow, that already sounds like fun and I don't even know what those names mean yet."

"Let me take them one at a time. I'll tell you just enough about them now to prepare you for the seminar. Then, at the seminar we will discuss each version in more detail and practice ways of breaking the patterns."

Elizabeth asked, "Can we start with Frozen TAG? That sounds intriguing."

"Actually, the first two sort of go together and the last two also go together, so I'll take them in pairs. And yes, we can start with the first pair."

"Okay, good," she responded gleefully.

Dr. Scott began by saying, "The one thing every child learns in a TAG-playing family is that it is terribly important not to be IT. And since there are two main ways to do this, they tend to develop in either one direction or the other."

"What are the two main ways to avoid being IT?" asked Joe.

"The first way is to be passive–to give the other people very little to work with. That way, they can't make you IT. It goes something like this:

'Hey, Dr. Scott, where do you want to go out to eat?'

'I don't care.'

or

'Hey, Dr. Scott, what did you do last night?'

'Nothing.'

or

'Hey, Dr. Scott, what are you going to do tomorrow?'

'I haven't decided yet.'

Joe flinched. "I've uttered those sentences myself. Does that mean I'm a passive person?"

Dr. Scott shook his head. "No, but it does mean that you have often chosen the passive route as a way to avoid being IT."

Joe nodded his agreement. "Yeah, that seems right."

Elizabeth asked, "So passivity is just a way to avoid being IT?"

"Sure. Like I said before, the beauty of being passive is that nothing is ever my fault. In other words, if I'm passive, I'm never IT."

Elizabeth looked uncertain. "But passive people always seem so unhappy and resentful."

"Oh, they are," Dr. Scott reassured her. "Remember, in TAG there is no way to win and no one is trying to be right. So, for a person coming out of a TAG-playing family, the fact that they are not winning is beside the point. All that matters is that they are not losing–that they are not IT."

Joe remarked, "So, getting it right–actually being happy–is never the goal."

"That's correct," Dr. Scott affirmed. "Every TAG player sacrifices even the possibility of being happy in order to avoid being IT. That's why, if you scratch the amiable surface of any 'laid-back' person, you will discover someone who is incredibly resentful and bitter—a person who is permanently angry about the fact that they never get any of the things they want."

Joe shook his head sadly. "Seems like a very high price to pay for not being IT."

"Oh, it's a very high price, indeed. A passive person has to avoid making any decisions, which means that they:

* procrastinate constantly, thereby creating a high level of chaos everywhere they go.

* avoid making any commitments, thereby creating a very small and boring life.

* never truly support anyone else, thereby letting down everyone in their life.

A very high price, for sure."

"Why did you name that game Frozen TAG?" Joe wondered.

"Frozen TAG is named after a game we used to play as kids," Dr. Scott explained. "It was a lot like regular tag, except that when you were tagged, you had to stay frozen in that position until one of the untagged kids came along and saved you."

Joe cocked his head and said, "So passive people stay frozen in one place, is that it?"

Dr. Scott replied, "Yes, until somebody else takes whatever action is necessary. And if that action goes badly, they get to blame somebody else. In other words, they're never IT."

Elizabeth smiled. "Here's how smart I'm getting. I bet they tend to marry people who are really controlling–whose comfort zone it is to make all the decisions and be in charge of all the action."

"Brilliant."

Joe inquired, "So, in the seminar we are going to learn how to recognize those TAG-players–the passive ones—and learn how to deal with them?"

"Yes. And you will also learn about the other type of person who comes out of TAG-playing families."

"The people who play Constant TAG?" Joe asked.

"Yes. Most of the other kids who come from TAG-playing families—the ones who don't play Frozen TAG—learn a different strategy to keep from being IT. They constantly make you IT, instead. My aunt Mildred is like that:

'Hi, Aunt Mildred.'

'Richard, I can't believe you wore such a casual shirt to the party.'

or

'Hi, Aunt Mildred.'

'I see you're finally on time for once.'

or

'Welcome to our home, Aunt Mildred.'

'Don't you think it's a little too late for your kids to still be up?'

That's Constant TAG," explained Dr. Scott. "No matter the occasion and no mater how polite I am, immediately she makes me IT. It took me a long time with Aunt Mildred to realize that it wasn't about me. She was just a person who dealt with her fear of being IT by constantly making somebody else IT."

Elizabeth shook her head sadly and said, "That sounds a lot like my family; always harping on other people's mistakes."

Joe agreed. "And a lot like my critical dad."

"Yes, both of your families used this strategy pretty often. In the seminar we will talk at length about how to break these two patterns, both at work and at home."

"Learning how to do that will be incredibly helpful to both Elizabeth and me."

Dr. Scott nodded. "Great. I'm thinking that learning how to deal with the other two forms of TAG I mentioned will be helpful to each of you, as well."

"What were they again?" Joe asked. "I forgot."

"That's okay. The third form of the game that we will address is the one I call Solitaire TAG, where people literally play TAG against themselves. They make the littlest mistake and then lash out at themselves, in their heads. It's good to know how to deal with people who do that and it's helpful to know how to interrupt that pattern when you do it yourself."

Joe grimaced and said, "Yeah, I do that one all of the time."

Dr. Scott nodded and then continued, saying, "The last form of TAG that we will talk about at this seminar is the one I call Team TAG. It's similar to the way little girls handle conflict. If Boy A is mad at Boy B, Boy A will have some direct interaction with Boy B. It might be an inappropriate interaction, of course, but the interaction will be between the two of them. On the other hand, if Girl A is mad at Girl B, how does she handle it?"

Elizabeth smiled. "I've seen this one a million times. She goes to Girl C and forms an alliance with her, in which they both agree that Girl B is awful and deserves to be treated terribly."

"That's exactly right," confirmed Dr. Scott. "I call that Team TAG–you and I both agree that everything is somebody else's fault and that they deserve to be treated badly."

She shook her head. "I know lots of women who still play that game. In fact, I have a girlfriend who calls me up every week just to tell me how big a jerk her husband is."

"I believe you," replied Dr. Scott. "The game is unbelievably common, especially among women. And here's the really weird thing about the game. In a purely TAG-playing family, this is the closest two people ever come to actually having a relationship. In her own odd way, your girlfriend is actually trying to bond with you in the only way she knows how."

Elizabeth's eyes opened wide. "So that's why she keeps on calling, even though she never takes my advice."

"Right. It's because she's not asking for your advice. She's asking you to agree that her husband is indeed a jerk, so that she feels less alone–like she has a friend."

Elizabeth looked a bit guilty. "I hate to admit it but I am I starting to avoid her calls."

"Yes, for a healthy person this is an uncomfortable way to interact, because it requires that you be negative—that you look for the bad side of the person who is IT. In the long run, it will always bring out your worst, most hurtful self."

Elizabeth replied, "That's why I'll be glad to learn how to drop that relationship."

"You may not have to," cautioned Dr. Scott. "There are ways to move the relationship in a healthy direction that may well work for you and your girlfriend. I will be covering that in the seminar."

"I'm looking forward to attending that seminar," she responded.

"And I look forward to having the two of you attend—it will move you along even faster than what we can do in these sessions."

"Any homework assignments in the meantime, doctor?" wondered Joe.

Dr. Scott nodded. "Two, actually. First, I would like each of you to identify the people and situations in which these four versions of TAG are most likely to occur in your life, so that you are prepared to maximize your learning at the seminar."

"Will do," he agreed.

"Also," Dr. Scott continued, "during our next session I would like do some strategizing as to where the two of you need to go from here. So, if you would both review all of your notes from our previous sessions and from the seminar, prior to our next session, our time together will be far more productive."

"Sounds like a plan," replied Joe.

"Good. I'll see you both at the seminar."

SUMMARY OF CHAPTER 7

- We break a TAG cycle gradually, by catching ourselves sooner and sooner in that cycle.
- There are only three ways to accomplish this: practice, practice, and more practice!
- People who often play Attacker and Fixer are likely to struggle with telling the truth.
- People who play Victim and Rehearsal are likely to struggle with hearing the truth.
- Often, one person in a couple struggles the most with telling the truth and the other struggles the most with hearing the truth.
- The rewards of breaking the game are immense–the instant we align ourselves with God's love, we are blessed in ways we could never have imagined.
- It is vitally important to celebrate any examples of breaking the game. These experiences are a critical step in the development of a truly intimate relationship.
- TAG-playing families produce children who tend to play either:
    - Frozen TAG ("If I'm passive, I don't give you anything to work with–there is no way for you to make me IT"). People who play this game generally offer few opinions, tend to procrastinate, avoid commitments, and never truly support others.
    - Or Constant TAG ("I will never have to be IT because I will always make you IT, from the very beginning of our conversation"). These people are seen by others as being very critical, have few friends, and tend to create a lot of trauma and drama.

- Solitaire is a game in which people play TAG against themselves.
- Team TAG is a game in which the tentative bond between two (or more) people is based solely on their agreement that a different person is IT. Gossip is a form of Team TAG.

EXERCISE #6

For each of the four versions of TAG that Dr. Scott described, please describe the situations in which (and the people with whom) you are most likely to play or to witness that particular game. Give a recent example of each.

1.) Frozen TAG (a persistent passivity, designed to avoid being made IT)

2.) Constant TAG (being negative and critical, in order to make other people IT)

3.) Solitaire TAG (a situation in which you or someone else are overly harsh with yourselves)

4.) Team TAG (in which two or more people agree that someone else is IT. Much of what is called gossip would fit here).

CHAPTER 8:

Alternatives to Frozen TAG and Constant TAG

"I would like to welcome all of you here today. As most of you know, I'm Dr. Scott.

I'm going to talk with you today about some of the ways in which you can deal with four of the most common versions of the game I call TAG–the ones I call Frozen TAG, Constant TAG, Solitaire TAG, and Team TAG. Before we get started, are there any questions?"

"Dr. Scott, is it okay to ask questions as we go?"

"Yes, Sheri, it's not only okay to ask, it will be beneficial to me and to the others. Otherwise it will be too much like a lecture, instead of a conversation—and that would be boring."

"Thanks."

"Any other questions? Yes, Elizabeth?"

"Are you going to ask us to draw upon our real-life examples?" she asked.

Dr. Scott replied, "I asked you to think of some examples before we started so that my talk today would make more sense to you. However, you will never have to share anything with the group unless you want to."

After pausing for a moment, he continued. "No other questions? Well, let's get right to it. In the Frozen TAG version of the game, either you or the other person consistently takes the passive route as a way to avoid being IT. How many of you can tell that you do this, as least some of the time?"

Many hands were raised.

Dr. Scott raised his hand, too, then commented, "Wow. Lots of us passive types here today. Great–then this part of the seminar should be especially helpful."

Just as he was about to begin, a hand was raised, so Dr. Scott stopped to ask, "Yes, Judy?"

"Is it true that passivity is always just a way to avoid being IT? I thought that I sometimes remained silent to avoid hurting someone else's feelings."

Dr. Scott smiled. "That's a good lead-in for me and I'm going to run with it. Before I teach you how to break this particular version of TAG there are two myths I need to dispel for you. The myth Judy just described is the first one."

"Why is that a myth?" Judy asked, sounding as if she may have felt a bit hurt.

"I have two responses," replied Dr. Scott. "First, I'm not telling you that you're IT. We have to be really clear with each other today. The fact that we may not always agree with one another does not mean that one of us has to be IT. Judy, are you okay with that?"

"Yes," she replied, with a smile. "I guess for a minute I didn't hear the truth."

"Way to be honest. Now here is why the sentence 'I didn't speak up because I didn't want to hurt their feelings' is a myth. One of my favorite writers once said, 'I used to pretend to myself that I was being nice because I did not want to hurt people. Now I know, though, that I was being nice because I was afraid–afraid of how the other person would react if I told the truth.' I think that's a powerful statement."

Judy winced and said, "That hits pretty close to home."

Dr. Scott nodded. "We pretend that we are protecting them, but who are we really protecting?"

"Ourselves," said Dennis. "Always ourselves."

"Exactly. And we are protecting ourselves from what?"

"From the reaction that would make us IT!" said Judy.

"Precisely," Dr. Scott affirmed. "And so we need to be honest with ourselves. When we rationalize our silence by saying 'I'm just being nice,' we are not telling our truth."

"We should always speak up, no matter what?" asked Joe, in his usual clarifying way.

"Actually, no. There are lots of perfectly good reasons for not speaking at certain times. Perhaps I am letting a more junior member of the group speak first, so they won't feel intimidated. Perhaps it's not my place to speak up–if I am the stepparent, for example, and need to let the biological parent handle a discipline situation, as we had agreed she would."

"Then there are times when it's okay to be passive?" Joe wondered.

Dr. Scott shook his head. "No, that's not what I said. I said there were times when it would be appropriate not to speak. That's not the same as being passive. In each of the situations I described, I would be actively choosing not to speak. In the first case, I would indeed speak, once it was my turn, and would attempt to address very directly what the junior member of the group had said. In the second example, I would not speak because I had already had an active conversation with the child's mom as to how to handle certain situations and I would be sticking to our prior agreement. Do you understand the difference?"

Joe nodded in understanding. "Yes, if I'm passive I deal with a situation by not dealing with it. In your examples, you did indeed deal with the situation–it's just that in dealing with it you did not need to speak at that moment."

"Thank you," replied Dr. Scott. "That's exactly what I meant. Was that clear to everyone else?"

"I'm not sure I got it," said Rachel. "Could you say it a different way?"

"Sure," said Dr. Scott happily. "It's always a lie to say, 'I'm choosing the passive route because I'm being nice to the other person.' Is that first part clear?"

"Totally," she replied.

"The second part is this: If we are to quit playing TAG, we must stop telling ourselves that lie and instead tell our truth. Are you still with me?"

"Yes," Rachel responded.

Dr. Scott concluded, "Finally, the fact that we are serious about telling the truth means that we do indeed speak up when it is our place or our turn to speak, but not until then. Part of what makes someone a good listener, for example, is that they don't speak out when they are supposed to be listening. They listen carefully, making sure they understand the situation, and then speak."

Rachel nodded her appreciation. "Thanks, that's a lot more clear, at least for me."

Dr. Scott said, "Good. Thanks for the question. Anything else that's unclear about the first myth?"

Danielle raised her hand and asked, "How do you know the difference between the lie of being passive and the wisdom of using discretion as to when to speak?"

"That same author I just quoted also said, 'The harder I have to work to justify my behavior, the more I can be sure there was something wrong with that behavior.' If you have to keep convincing yourself that what you did was right, it probably wasn't."

Danielle laughed. "I love little sayings like that."

Dr. Scott agreed. "Me too. It reminds me of something that I always think to myself–the truth is always simple."

"So what's the second passivity myth?" asked Carole.

"Thanks for helping me stay on track. The second myth is: 'Sometimes I don't speak up because I don't have an opinion–I just don't care,' or some words to that effect. That sentence is always a lie."

Lee practically jumped out of his seat. "How can you say that? Sometimes I really don't care."

Dr. Scott said, dryly, "Apparently, you cared about that sentence."

"Well, I thought the sentence was wrong," he said defensively.

Dr. Scott elaborated. "What I have come to understand, Lee, is that we actually have an opinion about everything that happens in front of us. Right now, for example, you have an opinion about what I just said, for sure. But you also have an opinion about the temperature in the room, the chair you're sitting in, and the clothes you're wearing. In fact, you even have an opinion about the clothes I'm wearing!"

"Yes, that's true, I guess," Lee acknowledged. "But some of the things you mentioned I don't care about very much."

Dr. Scott agreed. "Oh, I'm sure you're right about that. We all have big opinions about certain things and small opinions about other things; my point is, we always have opinions, even when we pretend that we don't."

Dennis smiled and said, "You make a good point, Dr. Scott. We have opinions about even the littlest things. But then why is it so upsetting to some of us to hear that?"

Dr. Scott smiled. "Because as soon as we acknowledge the truth about that, it blows the whole game."

"What game?" Dennis wondered.

"Frozen TAG," replied Dr. Scott.

"So as soon as we admit that we have all of these opinions, we can't play that version of TAG?"

"Exactly, Dennis. The game requires that we pretend to be 'laid-back'—to have no opinions about anything. But as soon as I tell my truth, instead of playing TAG, I have to admit that I have opinions, including some passionate opinions, about everything that happens around me all the time. And so I can't play the game."

Dennis nodded his head. "I get it—as soon as we admit that we have opinions about everything, we can no longer play Frozen TAG. But why would anyone want to play Frozen TAG in the first place?"

"For the same reason anyone ever plays a passive role in anything–to avoid being IT," Dr. Scott explained.

Dennis looked doubtful. "So people create this entire way of life, this whole 'laid-back' lifestyle, just to avoid being IT?"

Dr. Scott nodded his head and said, "Sadly, yes."

Lee raised his hand and said, "But some of the nicest people I know are what you would refer to as 'laid-back'–people who just go along with whatever is happening at the moment and never make a fuss. They are the kind of people that everybody likes."

"Let me share two thoughts with you, on that matter. First, 'everybody likes them,' as you say, but no one really knows them. Isn't that true?"

Lee looked uncomfortable, then replied, "I guess that's so."

"So they don't have any right relationships with anyone?"

"I guess not."

"So, then, Lee, can we agree that being 'laid-back' isn't a Christian's goal in life?"

As Lee and the people in the audience nodded their heads, Dr. Scott said, "And here's the second thing I want to say about that. When we call a person 'nice' we are only referring to what they don't do."

Dennis' wife, Janika, asked, "What do you mean, 'what they don't do'?"

Dr. Scott explained, "We call a person 'nice' because of what they don't do; for example, they don't interrupt, they don't raise their voice, they don't express strong opinions, they don't disagree, they don't act rudely, and they don't show up late."

"What's wrong with that?" wondered Janika.

"There's nothing wrong with any of those things," Dr. Scott reassured her. "I'm just trying to contrast being 'nice' with being good. Niceness is defined only by what you don't do; whereas goodness is an active, powerful force in its own right–it's God's love in action."

"Therefore, a person can be nice without being good?" asked Janika.

"Yes. In fact, being nice always gets in the way of being good, since goodness requires an active response. We are only nice because we are trying to avoid being IT. We are good, on the other hand, for an entirely different reason–because we want to have a powerful, positive impact upon our world. Do you see the difference?"

Janika tested her understanding. "So niceness is actually self-centered; whereas goodness is always others-centered."

"Right!" responded Dr. Scott, enthusiastically. "The first is based on the fear of making a mistake and the second is based on the passionate desire to do good–to live out a God-given vision. Of course, it is exactly that sort of vision that is discouraged in TAG-playing families, where having a vision just makes you a target."

Janika looked thoughtful. "I'm starting to understand why you were so hot on this topic. It's because people who play Frozen TAG really are frozen–they're not fully alive. And you want people to have big, exciting lives, filled with powerful relationships and a clear sense of God's purpose for their lives."

"Right!" confirmed Dr. Scott. "And a Frozen TAG-playing person will never achieve either one of those two marvelous goals you just described so beautifully."

Janika replied, "Dr. Scott, I think the greatest thing about you is that you are willing to fight for us, even before we have learned to fight for ourselves."

He blushed. "Thanks. You just made my day."

Lee asked, "So how do you break Frozen TAG?"

Dr. Scott turned toward Lee and said, "Good question. It depends on whether you are the person who plays it or are in a relationship with a person who plays it."

"What's the difference?" Lee wondered.

"If you are the person who plays it, your first goal has to be to break the first half of TAG–the 'nobody ever tells the truth' part," explained Dr. Scott.

"How do we do that?"

"Since everything in life always goes Think-Feel-Do, you have to start by getting your thinking right."

Lee nodded. "Now I get it. That's why you started by trying to explode certain myths. You wanted to challenge our old ways of thinking, so that we would get our minds right–so that we would get the 'thinking' part of Think-Feel-Do started in the right direction."

"That's exactly right," agreed Dr. Scott. "As long as a person believes, 'Oh, I'm just this way because I'm laid-back' or 'I'm just doing this to be nice,' they will remain stuck in their old behavior patterns because they are stuck in their old ways of thinking. Your thinking must be clear. You must know, for example, that you value intimacy over passivity."

Lee persisted. "So once we get our thinking right, what comes next?"

Dr. Scott continued, "Once your mind allows you to see things differently, you start the practice-practice-practice phase."

"And what do we start practicing?"

Dr. Scott asked, "Do you remember hearing me say that if I was going to teach a kid to play basketball, we would start with the lay-ups–the very simplest shot?"

"Yes," responded Lee simply.

Dr. Scott continued. "Well, the same approach applies here. I would ask that you start in the safest places, voicing your smallest opinions to the safest people in your life. When somebody that you trust asks where you would like to go out to eat, tell the truth. But remember, that's just YOUR opinion. Make sure to ask them for their opinion, too, before the two of you reach a decision. Practice with these micro situations before you begin to voice your opinions about more significant matters."

"Anything else?" Lee wondered, taking careful notes.

"Yes," replied Dr. Scott. "You can tell at least one or two or three people in your life–again the safest people–that you are going to be doing this. That way, they can support you when they see you striving to tell your truth and can also hold you accountable, by periodically asking you how the process is going."

Lee looked and sounded pleased. "This is good. What else can we do?"

Dr. Scott thought for a moment, then said, "Well, if you're a person who likes to write–a more introverted person, perhaps–you can begin to keep a journal, in which you record the thoughts that come to you each day. That way you will get to know yourself better, so that when people ask you what you think or how you feel about certain topics, you will actually know how to answer their questions."

Lee jotted down that idea too. "I'm a writer, so I like that idea. Any other suggestions?"

"If you are a more social learner, you could benefit from the fact that most communities have community education courses on assertiveness. If you are more of a one-on-one learner, you can also seek out a person in your area who has been specifically trained to help people transform their relationships."

Lee asked, "Do you ever work with people who are trying to quit playing Frozen TAG?"

Dr. Scott hesitated. "Well, I'm reluctant to do commercials, but there is a seminar of mine that anyone who has attended today's seminar can attend. It teaches people who previously played TAG how to build powerfully intimate relationships with all of the people in their lives.

"There is also a series of tapes and CDs that I recorded, called *My World.* The first CD in the set describes the game of TAG and the consequences of the game. The rest of the set starts with what I call 'Life's Most Dangerous Question,' which is 'What Do You Want?' and goes on to help the listeners answer that question and implement their own unique answers. It's all about helping you to create what I call a big life, which is a life filled with those things that are most important to you. People tell me these tapes and CDs have had a powerful impact on their lives. So if you are an audio learner, you might want to consider that approach."

Lee looked a bit overwhelmed. "Wow, that's a wealth of information. Thank you. You've given me hope."

"I'm glad to hear that," replied Dr. Scott. "Let's talk for a few minutes about how to break the Frozen TAG game if you are in relationship with someone who plays it, then we'll take a break."

Tamar said, "My best friend plays that game all of the time."

Dr. Scott turned to her and said, "Great. Give us an example of what she might do and then we'll talk about what you can do to break the Frozen TAG game she tends to play."

"Well, I'll ask her what she wants to do and she just says, 'I don't care. What do you want to do?' Or she will complain about a situation in her life, then not do anything about it."

Dr. Scott nodded. "Thanks for giving us a concrete place to begin our conversation. First, let me point out to any Frozen TAG players in the group how frustrated Tamar sounds. Please remember that sound, the next time you're tempted to tell yourself the lie that you are being passive for the good of someone else.

Secondly, I would point out to Tamar that before your friend can give up her part of this game, you have to be wiling to give up yours. All relationships are 50-50, after all, and we each play our part in every one of the dysfunctional patterns we create."

"Are you saying that I am responsible for her behavior?" asked Tamar indignantly.

"No, but I would gently suggest that you probably have other people in your life who act the same way your best friend acts."

"And so . . .?"

Dr. Scott continued, "And so, if you have attracted into your life a number of people who play a passive role in relationships, you have to ask yourself, 'Why do I keep setting up these types of relationships everywhere I go?' so you can begin to figure out your half of the pattern."

"And what is my half of the pattern?" Tamar asked, still sounding a little upset.

Dr. Scott replied, "Good question," and then waited.

Tamar smiled, and said with some reluctance, "Well, some people say I'm controlling."

"That's a start," he encouraged.

Beginning to talk more quickly, Tamar added, "And it's also true that I'm impatient; I like to make decisions quickly and move on. Some people say I'm impulsive or hyper but I like to think that I prefer action to sitting around discussing our options forever."

Dr. Scott asked, "Does it make sense to you that a person who likes to be in control and make rapid-fire decisions would tend to choose friends who passively allow her to run things, without a whole lot of input?"

Tamar smiled. "Yeah, that might make some sense."

"Then, as always, the first step in helping your friends become less passive is to change your thinking."

"Change it to what?" Tamar wondered.

"Well, right now your thinking is, 'Making a fast decision is better because I hate to sit around discussing our choices,' or something like that. Right?"

"Right."

Dr. Scott then pointed out, "And as long as that is what you believe, nothing will ever change."

"So what are you suggesting?" she wondered.

Dr. Scott said, "Right now you often get frustrated with your friends because they don't express their opinions. You think to yourself that the solution to your frustration is to make the decision yourself. So, you need to change your thinking to something like, 'Life will be a lot less frustrating when I slow down long enough to find out what they want,' or something along those lines."

"I can do that," she replied with confidence.

"Great. There's also one other change in your thinking that I might suggest would prove helpful to you," he added.

"What's that?" she asked, now clearly open to the feedback.

"The way you think right now is, 'I want to hurry up and get to the activities that I want to do.' But don't you also want to have relationships with those same people?"

"Of course," said Tamar, sounding a bit annoyed.

"But right now you don't," Dr. Scott pointed out.

Now Tamar was clearly upset. "How can you say that I don't have relationships with my friends?"

Dr. Scott continued on in the same tone. "How much do you know about what they want, what they like, or what their hopes and dreams are for that day and for their life?"

She responded hotly, "If I don't know those things it's because they don't tell me."

"Tamar, you're not IT," Dr. Scott gently pointed out.

"Yeah, yeah, I know," she replied, in obvious embarrassment.

Dr. Scott continued. "If your friends don't tell you what they want and what they like, then yes, it's partly because they don't speak up. But it is also partly because you don't ask them. And you don't ask them because you tell yourself that you hate to waste the time. But what if you decided that knowing your friends on a more intimate level was not a waste of your time?"

"It isn't a waste. I would love to know my friends better," she asserted.

Wanting to encourage her, Dr. Scott said, "Great. Remind yourself everyday that life will be far less frustrating and far more interesting if you slow down just long enough to ask your friends what they want. As soon as your thinking is clear about those two things, you can start the next practice-practice-practice phase."

"And what would I be practicing?" she asked.

"You would be practicing all of the gracious ways to not take 'no answer' for an answer."

Tamar looked confused. "You lost me there."

Dr. Scott nodded, then said, "Right now, when you ask your friend where she wants to go out to eat, what does she say?"

"She either doesn't answer at all or she says she doesn't care."

"And then what?" he prodded.

"Then we go to whatever restaurant I pick."

Dr. Scott nodded. "Exactly. See, you take 'no answer' for an answer. Your friend gives you no answer to your question, yet you act as if that response was acceptable to you–as if she had indeed answered the question."

"What should I do, instead?" asked Tamar, who by now was sincerely interested.

"First, remember that you actually want to know what she wants, for the reasons we have already discussed. Then, you refuse to accept 'no answer' for an answer."

"Like what?" she wondered.

"If she tells you she doesn't care, you say, without ever raising your voice, 'No, I really want to know what you think.' If she insists that it really doesn't matter to her, you say, 'But knowing what you think matters to me.' And you simply don't take one step forward until she has offered her opinion."

"That might take forever!" Tamar wailed.

Dr. Scott acknowledged the truth of what Tamar had said. "Yes, it probably will be slow at first. But she will get better and better at it with practice, just as you will get better and better at not taking 'no answer' for an answer."

Tamar smiled. "You know I'm impatient. Is there anything I can do to speed up the learning curve?"

"Absolutely. You can tell your friend ahead of time that you will be doing this. You can apologize to her for not having listened better in the past and then let her know that from now on you will be doing it differently. Acknowledging our part of the old pattern, first is always the right thing to do and it also will speed up the change process by a factor of 10."

She looked reluctant, then said, "I'm terrible at apologies. Do I have to apologize?"

Dr. Scott replied, "Since there are no victims, you don't have to do anything, least of all, apologize to your friend. But if you choose to do so, it will show her that it's safe for her to acknowledge her 50% too. Like all Frozen TAG players, she is deathly afraid of being IT, so if you take the rap at the front end, to let her know that she isn't going to get blamed, she will be more free to acknowledge her part of the problem, which means that she'll change a lot faster. Isn't that what you want?"

Tamar grinned. "For sure. Like I said, I'm impatient."

"Great. Go for it."

"Okay, I will," she promised.

Dr. Scott smiled his encouragement. "Good for you. Any last questions before we take a break?"

Juan raised his hand and asked, "Could you take a minute and summarize what you just taught Tamar?"

"Sure. Here are the six steps toward breaking Frozen TAG, when you are in a relationship with a person who plays that version of the game.

First, be clear what your 50% of the pattern is–in what way(s) is this game a part of your own comfort zone? In other words, be honest about the log in your own eye.

Second, be clear in your own mind what your reasons would be for doing your part differently. In other words, get a vision and get motivated.

Third, rehearse those reasons in your mind until they become a part of the way that you actually think. In other words, allow your new vision to radically change your thinking.

Fourth, once your mind is aligned with your true goals, refuse to take 'no answer' for an answer. Don't be aggressive, don't be loud, and don't be manipulative. Just let the other person know, consistently and persistently, that you really do want to know what they think. In other words, live with integrity, so that your actions match your goals.

Fifth, let them know, ahead of time, that you really want a closer relationship with them and that you will be asking more questions, so they know what to expect and so they can get on board with the program. This will reduce the amount of practice time that is needed.

Six, while you do this, make a point of apologizing for your previous contribution to the problem. It's the right thing to do and it also lets the Frozen TAG player know that they are not being blamed for the problem. This will allow them to quit making excuses for the past and move more boldly into the future."

"Thank you," Juan responded. "That was very clarifying."

"Great. Let's take a break, then we'll come back and have fun talking about how to break Constant TAG."

"Welcome back," said Dr. Scott. "How many of you have at least one person in your life who plays Constant TAG–someone who begins every conversation with a negative or critical comment, just to make sure that they're not IT?"

Everyone raised their hands.

"Wow! Then this will be interesting to all of you. There are at least three ways to deal with Constant TAG players. The first is the most fun, which is why I'll start there. Who can give me an actual recent quote from a Constant TAG player?"

Karin raised her hand. "Yesterday my husband Erik and I went to visit my in-laws. As soon as we got to the door, my mother-in-law said, 'The flowers you sent for Aunt Amelia's funeral looked terrible by the day of the funeral.' I was so taken aback that I don't even remember what I said."

"If you were like most people, you responded by disagreeing, apologizing, or defending yourself, all of which are ways to continue the game of TAG."

"What should I have done?" asked Karin.

Dr. Scott stopped and said, "The word 'should' is still a way to play TAG. Do you understand that?"

"Yes," Karin replied, "it's about judgment and about not doing things wrong, which is what TAG is all about."

"Precisely," agreed Dr. Scott.

"So how could I have handled that situation more effectively?" she asked, perfectly.

"Good question," Dr. Scott replied. "My first strategy is both the right thing to do and also clever, which makes it fun. Whenever I come in contact with a Constant TAG player, my first strategy is to find whatever factual thing they said that I can agree with and then invite them into a 'we' solution. For example, in that situation I might say, 'Yeah, they were past their prime, for sure. What do you think we should do next time to make sure that doesn't happen again?' "

Karin grinned. "Oh, you're right, that will be fun."

Dr. Scott agreed, then elaborated. "It is fun and it is also beautifully functional, for two reasons. First, TAG players always act like they are telling the truth but they're not. Your mother-in-law's real message was not about the flowers. The real message was 'you're bad, you're bad, you're bad,' which is not true. The truth is that you are God's precious child. So by saying something like, 'yes, they were past their prime,' you are re-focusing the conversation on the flowers, instead of on you. And she can't object, since she brought them up and is busy pretending that those flowers are indeed the topic of the conversation.

"Secondly, it breaks the game by creating a team. TAG players feel they are alone and make everyone else around them feel the same way. So, by suggesting a 'we' solution, you invite her out of the cold and onto your team."

Karin asked, "What if she responds by saying, 'I don't know how to keep that from happening again,' or something crabby like that?"

Dr. Scott smiled, teasing her. "Oh, I don't think that's an 'if,' I think that's a 'when.' That's pretty much guaranteed to happen, don't you think?"

"Yes. So, what could I do then?"

Dr. Scott advised, "Stick with the game plan, no matter what. Agree with what's factual and suggest a 'we' approach to the problem. You could say, 'Yeah, I'm not sure either, right now. We'll have to give that one some thought before the next occasion arises,' or something like that.

Karin laughed. "I am so excited about this. I'll never have to play TAG with her again."

"Right. She'll never have that kind of power over you again. Instead, you will experience the liberating power of God's love. And here's the really funny part. At first, she won't know what to do with you, since you won't be playing by her usual rules. That by itself will be fun to observe. But it gets even better. Eventually, she may well decide that you're her favorite of all the in-laws. And you'll smile to yourself every time you see her being so nice to you."

Luis asked, "How would I take the same approach when my Constant TAG brother says to me, 'The rest of you aren't visiting Dad often enough,' whenever I do go to see my dad?"

"Yes, it probably would be good to look at the visitation patterns we're in now and sit down as a family to discuss that. How do you think we should organize that?"

"Got it. Gently agree, with no defending, and ask about a team solution. That's brilliant."

Dr. Scott smiled his thanks. "And it will work every time. But please understand, 'work' doesn't mean the Constant TAG player will necessarily become an enjoyable person to be around. Your goal is not to change them. Your goal is to quit playing TAG with them. Is that clear?"

"To me, that's very clear," responded Luis.

"Good," encouraged Dr. Scott. "I would like to point out to you that whereas breaking the Frozen TAG game requires an increased willingness to tell the truth, breaking Constant TAG requires an increased willingness to hear the truth. Karin, do you understand what I mean by that?"

"I think so," she replied. "To break Frozen TAG, we have to get better at saying what we think and asking for what we want. But to break Constant TAG, we have to get better at remembering that the things critical people say are not actually about us."

Dr. Scott said, "Right. Because if you had responded to your mother-in-law's criticism of the flowers by defending yourself, by explaining why you did what you did, or by apologizing, you would be acting as if her comments were indeed about you."

Karin nodded. "But now I understand that her comments are not about me. She's just a negative, Constant TAG-playing person who is afraid of being IT. So she starts every conversation off with a critical statement, as her way of making somebody else IT."

"And why does she do that?" coached Dr. Scott.

"Because that's what she does."

"And who is that about?" he continued.

"It's about her and her fear," Karin responded.

"Perfect," Dr. Scott replied. "Once you understand that, you are free to choose a different response. You might even be able to summon up a compassionate one, once you truly understand how afraid she is and how much her entire life is lived in fear."

Karin brightened. "That's a liberating thought."

"Great." he said to Karin. "It's a great example of what Christ meant when he talked about loving our enemies." Then, speaking to the entire group, he added, "Here's another liberating thought. No one can make me be IT. Not ever."

Luis looked thoughtful. "Never?"

"Never," restated Dr. Scott, firmly. "How many kids does it take to play tag?"

Luis responded, "At least two. One who is chasing and one who is running to avoid being caught."

Dr. Scott nodded. "And as soon as either child quits playing, what happens to the game?"

Luis nodded in understanding. "It ends, instantly."

The doctor agreed. "That's precisely my point. And as long as I am not playing, I can't be IT."

Luis looked excited. "I like that. That's going to be my goal in life–to never be IT!"

Dr. Scott was pleased with the strength of Luis' conviction. "Here are some other ways to accomplish that, when you are in the presence of a person or a group of people who play Constant TAG.

My second strategy is to simply start a different, more positive, conversation. So if my mother-in-law says, 'The flowers you sent for Aunt Amelia's funeral looked terrible by the day of the funeral,' I might respond by saying, 'That really was a beautiful service, wasn't it?' or something like that."

"That's devious," laughed Joe. "When my Constant TAG co-worker says, 'At the rate you're going, the report you're writing will never be ready in time for the meeting,' what could I say back?"

"That is an important meeting, isn't it? It will be interesting to see how things turn out."

Joe grinned. "I love that. And it's a great example of how we don't have to get pulled into other people's TAG games, just because they start the conversation there."

"That's right," said Dr. Scott. "It's like Luis says, you'll never have to be IT again, if you use either of these strategies."

Elizabeth smiled at Joe's excitement and then turned to Dr. Scott and asked, "But what if Joe and I are at my family's house and people all around us are playing TAG?"

"Then it's time for my third strategy–the one I call 'Yes, I see that too.' "

"What does that mean?" she asked.

Dr. Scott elaborated. "If Rose and I are at a function where people are playing TAG all around us, I just touch her leg if she's sitting by me or smile at her across the room and nod my head, like 'yes, these people really are playing TAG like crazy.' That way, the two of us are on each other's team. Knowing that breaks the game of TAG for us, since in TAG you are always alone. Then, knowing I'm okay, I turn to the person next to me and ask them a personal question–something that will allow the two of us to have a non-TAG conversation."

Elizabeth gave Dr. Scott a grateful smile. "Thank you, that's helpful. Joe and I will need to work on being a strong team when we visit my family."

Dr. Scott returned the smile. "Good. In the meantime, until you get stronger, spend as little time with them as you can."

"Got it," she responded.

"Let's go eat lunch and then this afternoon we will talk about Solitaire and about Team TAG."

SUMMARY OF CHAPTER 8

- Two of the myths that underlie the game of Frozen TAG are:
- "I am being nice to protect the other person." In reality, being nice is a self-protective thing that we do to avoid being IT. It is never the same as being good because goodness is others-centered; it is about being a positive force in the lives of other people. If you read the scriptures carefully, you will often see Jesus being good but you will never see him being nice.
- "I don't care," or "I don't have an opinion." These statements are never true, since we all have opinions about everything around us. These lies, often used by "laid-back" people, are lies we tell in order to avoid expressing an opinion or making a decision. In other words, passive people pretend not to care, to avoid being judged for their opinions or decisions—to avoid being IT.
- Being passive and choosing to remain silent at the moment are not the same thing. The first is a knee-jerk, unthinking reaction that I exhibit everywhere I go and the second is a conscious decision that I make, in order to achieve a specific and positive objective.
- If you are the person playing Frozen TAG, you can break the game by:

    Changing your thinking (i.e., replacing the myths with the truth). Possible truths are: "I do indeed have opinions," "I want people to know me," and "there is more to life than not being wrong."

    Starting to express your smallest opinions to the people who are closest to you.

    Telling those people that you will be speaking up, so that they can both support you and hold you accountable.

Writing in your journal, as a way of getting to know yourself better.

Taking a community ed class or visiting with a relationship specialist.

Attending the next relationship seminar and/or purchasing the tapes or CDs that were described in the chapter.

- If a person in your life plays the game, you can:

Be honest with yourself about your 50% of the pattern.

Be clear with yourself as to why you would want the situation to be different.

Rehearse those reasons until your thinking changes.

Refuse to take "no answer" for an answer.

Let the other person know that you want a closer relationship with them.

Start by acknowledging your part of the problem, so that they will know they're not IT.

- In order not to be pulled into the game of Constant TAG, you can:

Agree with some factual part of what was said and then suggest a "we" approach to the problem ("Yes, those flowers were sort of wilted. How do you think we could keep that from happening in the future?")

Start a different, more positive conversation ("Yes, that will be a very important meeting. What do you think will be the outcome?")

- If a group is playing, turn to your partner (either verbally or with an agreed upon gesture) and indicate, "Yes, I see that, too." Once you know you are not alone, strike up a personal conversation with the person next to you.

EXERCISE #7

1.) Which of the suggested approaches will you use to reduce the frequency with which you play Frozen TAG? To whom will you be accountable for these changes?

2.) Give a recent example of a time when someone else in your life played Frozen TAG with you and then walk through the six steps outlined in the text, to clarify the ways in which you can break that game from your end.

3.) Who are some of the people who are likely to play Constant TAG with you?

4.) Give an example of a recent interaction with one of these people and then write down at least two non-TAG playing responses to that interaction, drawing upon the strategies described by Dr. Scott.

CHAPTER 9:

Alternatives to Team TAG and Solitaire

Dr. Scott opened the afternoon session by saying, "In this portion of the seminar I get to talk with you about Team TAG, which, as you all know, is the version of TAG where the person to whom you are speaking makes someone else IT and then invites you to do the same. It's a common form of communication in TAG-playing families and is also the way elementary school girls 'resolve' their conflicts."

Isaac said, "I know lots of families in which it's not only the little girls who interact like that–it's the whole family. In my family, my mother is always calling me up to tell me why she is so upset with my brother. I'm sure she does the same thing when she calls my brother, only then I'm the one who is IT, instead. What an insane way to converse!"

Dr. Scott nodded. "Yes, it seems an odd way of interacting, until one realizes that it actually makes perfect sense, from a TAG perspective."

Isaac shook his head. "How could such craziness make sense?"

Dr. Scott explained, "We all have a real need to be connected to others–to be in right relationship. But in TAG, no one trusts anyone else enough to be vulnerable with them. After all, I know perfectly well that if you were IT, you would do everything in your power to tag me. So, vulnerability is out. That means the only way for two people to connect, at least temporarily, is for them both to be invulnerable—for them both to be safe from being IT. And in TAG, what is the only way for two people not to be IT?"

Isaac smiled. "To make a third person IT."

"Right," agreed Dr. Scott. "As long as you and I agree that your poor loser of a brother is IT, it's safe for us to be connected. As soon as he isn't IT, all bets are off and we are back to not being able to trust each other—we're back to creating distance."

Isaac nodded his head, reluctantly. "I guess that does make sense, in a rather distorted way. How do we break this version of TAG—how do I handle my mom differently, when she calls?"

"Good question. Where do we always need to start?"

Isaac responded instantly. "With our thinking. Think-Feel-Do."

"Right. And when your mom calls, what are you thinking?"

Isaac grimaced. "Oh, no, not again! How can I get out of this conversation?"

Dr. Scott said, "That thinking certainly is both clear and understandable. Are you willing to think differently about this?"

"I would be thrilled to find a different way to think about those calls," Isaac replied.

Dr. Scott suggested, "Would you be willing to say to yourself, 'Hey, here's a chance to have a real conversation with my mom,' or words to that effect?"

Isaac shrugged. "Sure, if it would change anything."

"I guarantee it will. That's your first step toward real change."

"Okay, I'll change my thinking about the calls," Isaac promised.

Dr. Scott continued. "Great. Here's the second way in which you can radically alter those conversations. When you allow your mom to lead the conversation, who is the conversation always about?"

"My brother, my dad, the doctor, whoever has messed up lately," he smiled.

"In other words," Dr. Scott pointed out, "it is always about someone who is not actually in the conversation–that's the nature of Team TAG, right?"

"Absolutely," he agreed.

"As long as you either argue with her or agree with her, the conversation will continue to be about someone else–the two of you will continue to play Team TAG?"

Isaac shook his head in disgust. "For sure–that's what I always do and that's how our talks always go—they're so predictable and so boring."

"I understand," Dr. Scott responded sympathetically. "You're right. The interactions in any game of TAG really ARE incredibly predictable–that's why the game is so boring. But once your mind is clear and you actively choose to do it differently, you can change the entire course of the conversation simply by having it be about anyone who is actually in the conversation."

Isaac looked confused. "So . . ."

Dr. Scott continued, "So, in this case, you could either ask your mom a question about herself or you could share a piece of fun information about yourself."

"I get it. I just make the conversation revolve around us, instead of allowing her to choose the topic of the conversation."

"Precisely," affirmed Dr. Scott. "It's a great example of what I mean when I say that to break TAG we must be gracious (good) but we can't be polite (nice). Polite people always go where you lead them. So they can easily be pulled into Team TAG conversations. Gracious people, on the other hand, gently take control of the conversation and move it in a more loving direction. It's a perfect example of the difference between nice and being good."

Isaac tested his understanding by saying, "So I need to be more proactive and less reactive."

Dr. Scott nodded emphatically and said, "Yes, and you don't even need to be obvious about it; you can take the conversation in a far more personal direction, without totally changing the topic. You do it in two steps that I call 'connect and then lead.' For example:

'Your loser brother is in jail again.'

'I'm sorry to hear that. How are you doing with that, mom?'

'Your father forgot his friend's name today and it was really obvious.'

'I did that once, too. That was really embarrassing for me.'

'That plumber didn't fix that faucet right.'

'That must be really frustrating for you. What are you going to do?'

'My allergies are bothering me and the doctor hasn't helped me at all.'

'Mine are kind of acting up too. What have you tried so far?'

'My brother and sister aren't sharing the family cabin the way they should.'

'That does sound unfair. How would you like it to be?'

Do those examples help to explain what I mean?" asked Dr. Scott.

Isaac replied, "Yes, they're very clear, I think. Basically, I can just stay on the same topic, express concern, and then either ask a question about how the situation is affecting her or share a reaction of my own. Suddenly, no more Team TAG!"

Dr. Scott smiled. "Thank you. That was a perfect summary of my 'connect, then lead' philosophy."

Isaac's wife, Isabelle, spoke. "That's all fine, but what if she stills tries to keep complaining?"

Dr. Scott replied, "Again, I'm sure that won't be an 'if.' It's bound to happen, isn't it, Isaac?"

"Yes," he agreed, "it's a certainty, since playing Team TAG is the only thing she knows how to do."

Dr. Scott began by saying, "If your mom responds in that way, stay with the same approach. Let's say that you do ask mom what she's tried, with respect to her allergies, as a way to get her to talk about herself instead of her doctor. And let's say she goes right back to focusing on the doctor, saying, 'Nothing that quack has suggested has worked.' You simply repeat the approach, even more clearly. 'Yeah, our allergies are no fun. But I really wanted to know what you've tried so far, so that I won't waste my time on those approaches." At that point, she is unlikely to keep talking about the doctor, but even if she does, you simply say, 'Mom, you're the one I love. I want to hear about you, not about the doctor.' As long as you refuse to play Team TAG, it simply can't happen."

Isabelle persisted. "But what if she STILL keeps doing it?"

Dr. Scott smiled. "You're not trying to make his mother IT, are you?"

Isabelle blushed and said, "Maybe. She drives me crazy."

"If that was true, what would it mean?" asked Dr. Scott.

"It would mean that I was somehow making it about me," Isabelle acknowledged.

"Right," agreed Dr. Scott. "And who is it actually about?"

"His mom."

Dr. Scott continued her thought, "His mom, who desperately wants to connect to someone and doesn't know how."

Isabelle nodded, with the first glimmer of compassion. "I understand. She's not really the bad one. She just lacks skills."

"Skills which she will actually acquire eventually, as long as Isaac keeps doing as I have suggested," Dr. Scott pointed out.

Isabelle brightened. "That's a hopeful thought."

Dr. Scott concluded, "So, to answer your question, without the TAG component, I would say a little prayer for her in my heart, mention the time, say that I had to get going, without giving a reason, and hang up. And next time I would give her another chance, while continuing to use my newly acquired anti-TAG tools. And how many times would I do this? Seventy times seven."

Isaac grinned and said, "I like that. I give her several chances to have a far more interesting conversation with me, I discontinue the conversation if she refuses my invitations, and I relentlessly try again later. And no matter what, I will not be a part of one of those old interactions."

"Exactly," encouraged Dr. Scott. "See, all of the 'what ifs' in the world really don't matter. You just have to be really clear in your own mind–you're never going to be in one of those Team TAG conversations again."

Angelica excitedly stood up and said, "I love this concept. But what do you do if everyone in your family plays that game?"

Dr. Scott smiled and asked, "Is this a hypothetical question?"

Angelica made a face at him and said, "You know it isn't."

Dr. Scott replied, "On a more serious note, I'm all about starting at the safest place and taking things one piece at a time. So, if I was you, I would talk to my honey about who in the extended family might be most open to doing it differently and then ask that person or that nuclear family to dinner. While we were out to dinner I would tell them that I wanted to have a closer relationship with them, a relationship in which there was no need to play TAG. After I had cultivated that relationship, I would start slowly expanding that circle. It takes time but it's very likely to have a positive impact on the family dynamics. Just make sure you don't play Team TAG against the family members who are not yet in the circle."

Angelica nodded thoughtfully. "That's a good point. It would be easy to fall into that."

Dr. Scott replied, "Right. Then, instead of being the solution, you would just be re-creating the TAG problem that you were trying to eliminate."

"Yeah, I surely don't want to be doing that."

Dr. Scott turned to address the whole group, saying, "I would ask that you all notice this: each of the new approaches I have suggested start with the decision to be in charge of the process. The general suggestion that Isaac talk about himself or his mother, the specific 'connect and then lead' approach, the family-change strategy I suggested to Angelica, or my reminder not to use that strategy as a way to play Team TAG against the others, all share this one trait–they break TAG by leading.

Polite people follow, gracious people lovingly lead. Not for the sake of their own ego but for the sake of the relationship. Because here's the deal: if you don't lead, the interaction patterns will never change. And that would be a terrible loss, for you and for them."

Angelica nodded. "I like that way of thinking about it. We're not trying to break TAG just for ourselves. We are trying to make other people's lives better, too."

"That's exactly right. And that's what it means to be good, instead of nice. It means that we are actively striving to improve our lives and the lives of all those around us, to whom we are connected through God's love. We break TAG as a way to honor our God. Let's take our last break and then we will come back and talk about the game I call Solitaire."

"In our final session for today, I want to talk to you about the version of TAG I call Solitaire. In this game, either you or the other person is unduly hard on themselves, whenever a mistake is made. Solitaire players make themselves IT all of the time.

If you want to know whether or not you belong to this group, just look back to the last mistake you made and then re-play the comments that ran through your head. If you called yourself names, cursed, told yourself how stupid you were, or got really upset, chances are you play Solitaire pretty often.

If you want to know whether a person in your life plays Solitaire, just notice what happens when someone volunteers to help them, pays them a compliment, or gives them a gift. If they automatically refuse the help, blow off the compliment, or appear uncomfortable with the gift, chances are they play Solitaire too."

Ramona looked sorrowful and said, "You just described both my uncle and my nephew. I would love to know how I could help them. Can I?"

"Yes, there are a number of ways you can help. For today, I am going to talk about three very specific things you can do to help people who play Solitaire. Then, in the future seminar on parenting, we will cover this topic in much greater detail."

Ramona replied, "Thanks. I am open to any suggestions you may have, both now and in the future."

Dr. Scott began, "My first suggestion is this: you can be very intentional about observing The 90-10 Rule when you are with them. Make a point of seeing them through God's eyes—seeing everything great about them and letting them know you see it. But keep it brief–don't embarrass them by going on and on about it. After all, these are people who are uncomfortable receiving compliments at all, so don't overdo any one bit of praise."

Ramona hesitated, then asked, "What if they won't receive the praises I give them?"

Dr. Scott smiled. "You probably can guess, by now, my response to that."

She looked confused for a second, then said, "Right, it's not an 'if.' It's a sure thing."

"Yes. This will indeed happen. And what are the only three ways to get better at anything?"

"Practice, practice, and more practice," she replied.

"Right, in both directions," he reminded her. "Give yourself some time to get better at seeing and praising their precious self and give them some time to practice getting better at receiving that praise."

Ramona nodded. "Got it. What's your second suggestion?"

Dr. Scott replied, "If, after having had time to practice, they still are not any better at receiving your praises, then you might want to say to them, at a time when no one else is present, that it is hurtful to you when they don't accept your compliments."

Ramona shook her head. "Wouldn't that be upsetting to them?"

Dr. Scott said, in all seriousness, "I would hope so. But then, I understand that the goal of a Christian is to be gracious, not polite–to be good, not to be nice."

Ramona remained unconvinced. "Why would it be all right to upset them?"

"Wouldn't you be upset to discover you had been and continued to be hurtful to a family member?" asked Dr. Scott.

"Yes, of course," she answered.

Dr. Scott continued to prompt her. "But wouldn't you also want to know that your behavior had been hurtful, so you could change that behavior?"

"For sure," she agreed.

"So, it would be a loving act to tell you?" he asked.

"Yes, if the intent was to be of help to me."

Dr. Scott concluded, "Well, a Solitaire person acts that way, in part, because they don't realize the impact of their behavior upon others. And you're right—it would be a loving act to tell them about that impact, as long as you were doing it for <u>their</u> benefit and not just to make someone other than yourself IT."

Ramona nodded. "I get it. Sharing that information, if it was for the right reason, would be upsetting to them but would also be very helpful to them."

"Yes," Dr. Scott replied, "if they allowed themselves to hear it."

"And that decision would be about them, not about me," she said.

Dr. Scott grinned. "Ramona, you're getting smarter by the minute."

"Thanks. What's the last of your three suggestions?"

Dr. Scott hesitated a moment, then said, "This one is relevant for everyone, I suppose, but it is particularly relevant for people who have children or young relatives. Although we can also help to break the Solitaire game by observing The 90-10 Rule, as I've suggested, the single best weapon against Solitaire is this: to pay loving attention to the person when they are not doing anything."

Ramona looked puzzled. "I'm not sure I'm following you."

Dr. Scott elaborated. "In the case of my daughter, Sandi, for example, it's fine that I go to her violin concerts, attend her school events, and praise her academic performance. But it is critically important that I plunk down beside her, put my arm around her, and tell her how blessed I am to have her, when she is just sitting on the couch watching TV."

"Why is that so critical?" she asked.

"Because in Solitaire, as in any form of TAG, people don't realize that they are precious. They think their performance is all that matters—that they are only worth what they produce. That's why mistakes are so devastating–they leave a Solitaire person feeling worthless."

Ramona looked sorrowful. "That's a sad thought."

"Yes," agreed Dr. Scott, "it is sad. And your response is a great example of the compassion we feel for others, as long as we are not playing TAG."

"Right."

"So," he continued, "in Solitaire, the person believes their performance is what matters. But if I express affection for Sandi when she is just watching TV, the message is loud and clear–'I love you, not your performance.' And that very godly message is the best possible way to break the game of Solitaire."

Ramona beamed. "That's an inspiring thought. I am going to put that into practice this week. I'll bet every person in my life needs more of that godly perspective from me."

Dr. Scott agreed. "I'm sure that's true for all of us."

Elizabeth asked, "What are some of the ways in which we can send that message to the people in our life?"

Dr. Scott gathered his thoughts, then replied, "Any form of affectionate touch sends the other person the message that they are precious. So does listening intently, spending time with them, asking simple questions, seeking their opinions, and re-telling inside jokes."

Elizabeth nodded her appreciation. "That gives me some concrete things to work on. Thanks."

"Glad to help. Any more questions, before we move on to talking about how to break the game of Solitaire when you are the one playing it?"

When no one raised their hand, Dr. Scott said, "Anything that helps you to realize that love is what you actually need and that you are indeed loved will help you to break the game. Now, please understand, this means you will have to give up your search for approval."

"Why is that?" Joe wondered.

Dr. Scott explained. "Because you can't seek both love and approval—they are mutually exclusive. When we seek approval we put out a false self, in order to trick people into liking us. When we seek love, on the other hand, we must put out our true self, and allow people to make up their own minds about loving us. Solitaire is based on gaining approval for our performance, or, more to the point, about avoiding disapproval. The Christian life, on the other hand, is about receiving God's love, which is independent of our performance."

"Got it. How do we get better at receiving His love, instead of seeking after approval?"

Dr. Scott continued. "All of the best ways to break our obsessive thirst for approval require that we pay careful attention."

"Attention to what?" Joe wondered.

"To all of the love that people already are trying to give to us. We mistakenly believe that we need to manipulate people into loving us, but that's a lie. They already do love us and they show that love to us in many different ways every day. That's why our only job is to pay attention—to see that love and to accept it for what it is."

Luis looked doubtful. "How can you be so sure all of that love is happening in my life?"

Dr. Scott explained, "Because there isn't anyone in this room who doesn't receive at least 50 messages every day, telling them that they are loved and that they matter."

"Then I don't think I've hit my quota yet for today," Luis joked.

Dr. Scott smiled. "Actually, I know for a fact that you have already exceeded your quota."

"What do you mean?"

Dr. Scott elaborated. "Already today, God met you in your prayer time, many different people smiled at you as you walked past, group members listened intently to you as you spoke, individuals made eye contact with you during your follow-up conversations with them, your wife attended this seminar because her relationship to you matters so much to her, and your honey frequently held your hand while the two of you were sitting there. People you don't even know held the door open for you when you arrived, made a space for you on the freeway while you were driving here, and prayed for you prior to this seminar. The eyes of your children lit up this morning when they saw you, the dog wagged her tail excitedly when she heard you coming, and your neighbor waved to you when you went out to get the newspaper. Have I reached 50 yet?"

"I think we might have passed that up a while back," joked Luis.

Dr. Scott smiled. "Yes, I think so."

Elizabeth said, "This discussion reminds me of a conversation Joe and I had with you early on in the counseling process, to the effect that God's love binds all of us together, whether we realize it or not."

Dr. Scott agreed, passionately. "That's exactly the point. We don't need to invent those sacred connections–we just need to honor them. And honoring them requires only that we notice them, receive them, and be grateful for them. That's why I always say that the two most important words in the Christian vocabulary are 'yes' and 'thank you.' "

Luis nodded. "So I don't need to make people love me. I just need to accept ('yes') the fact that people already do love me and then appreciate ('thank you') all of the ways they try to show me that they do."

"Right," confirmed Dr. Scott. "And just so you know what to look for, you should know that the love we receive tends to come in one of six forms: greetings, affectionate touch, compliments, listening, thoughtful gifts, and offers to help."

Elizabeth asked, "How do we get better at receiving these six different forms of love?"

"I go into this in more detail in the set of tapes and CDs I mentioned before, so that those who want to hear more about this can do so. For now, I will mention five things you can do.

The first is really simple. Notice how happy people are to see you. While they are joyfully greeting you, remind yourself that you haven't done anything yet. And accept the fact that since they are pleased to see you, even though you have not yet performed in any way, it must be you that they love, not your performance.

Elizabeth smiled. "What do I need to do to let that soak in?"

Dr. Scott responded by saying, "That's exactly what you need to do. Allow yourself to be in the present moment and to notice how good it feels to have them greet you. Look closely at their face and see how their smile conveys love for you. If they hug you, notice how great it feels to have their arms around you. Soak in the experience like a sponge and you will be changed forever."

Elizabeth replied, "That does sound great. That approach will make the experience so much better for me."

Dr. Scott nodded. "And for them, too, of course, since we're all connected."

"That is so right," Elizabeth agreed.

Dr. Scott continued. "The second thing you can do is this. When you receive a compliment, you need to make eye contact, smile, nod your head, and say 'Thank you; that means a lot to me.' Don't blow it off, don't minimize it, and don't act as though you don't deserve it. Those are just ways to play Solitaire. Accept the compliment and the love behind it–that way you won't need to settle for approval, which is just a cheap substitute for God's love. Instead, you will be receiving the real thing."

"Why is that so hard for so many of us?" Elizabeth wondered.

"Because in TAG-playing families, compliments don't happen, for reasons that we discussed previously. People from those families don't get many opportunities to practice receiving compliments. And all of us are uncomfortable with things that are new to us."

"So it will get easier with time?" she asked, hopefully.

"Yes," the doctor reassured her, "with time and with practice, practice, and more practice."

Elizabeth just smiled.

"The third thing you can do," continued Dr. Scott, "is to appreciate ignorance."

Elizabeth laughed. "Then Joe should love me like crazy right now because I have no idea what you're talking about!"

Dr. Scott laughed as well, and said, "By that I mean, in any conversation, the listener's most helpful tool is their ignorance. Let's say that a person says to me, 'I'm having a hard day.' If I assume that I know what they mean, I will respond by saying something like, 'I know what you mean,' and that will be the end of the conversation."

Elizabeth responded, "I've had lots of conversations like that."

"But if a person loves us," Dr. Scott explained, "they use their ignorance. Instead of assuming they know what we mean, they ask, 'How come?' or something like that."

"So when a person uses their ignorance and asks me a question. . ."

Dr. Scott completed her thought. "Then you need to see it as the loving act that it is and answer the question fully. A person who uses their ignorance when they are with you is a person who truly wants to get to know you. Answering their questions fully is a way to let them get to know you, which is a prerequisite for them loving you."

Elizabeth looked appreciative. "This is SO helpful. What's the fourth thing I can do?"

Dr. Scott continued. "The fourth thing you can do is to accept the small gifts people give to you, including cards, notes, and presents on your birthday."

"I've always had a hard time with that," Elizabeth noted.

Dr. Scott nodded. "Lots of people do. If you struggle with this, just imagine you have a friend whom you dearly love. Their birthday is coming up and you want to buy them the perfect present. You give it a lot of thought and finally come up with a truly inspired idea. You shop at many different stores to find exactly what you want, wrap it beautifully, and drive all the way across town to bring it to your friend's house. When they open the door, see you standing there with your perfect gift, and say, 'No, I can't take that,' and close the door, how do you suppose you would feel?"

Elizabeth clearly understood his point. "I would feel very hurt."

Dr. Scott agreed. "Yes, I am sure you would. And my point is this: It is not just okay to accept gifts gracefully. It is terribly important to do so. To be anything less than a gracious receiver is to be very hurtful to the giver. If you would really think about it, you would understand that being a gracious receiver is actually a form of giving."

Elizabeth concluded, "So, as you are always saying, in the world that God actually created, not the crazy one we make up in our heads, when we work on doing what is right for us, it benefits everyone around us, as well."

"Exactly. Because we are all connected through God's love. I wanted you all to understand that, because it will be easier for you, when you receive a gift, to just smile and say thank you."

Elizabeth was still a bit unclear. "But what if you don't deserve such a gift?"

Dr. Scott said simply, "You don't."

"What?!"

"If you had earned it," he asked, "in what way would it be a gift?"

Elizabeth smiled and nodded her head thoughtfully. "You do have a way of altering a person's perspective."

Dr. Scott smiled in acknowledgment of the compliment. "Thanks. How could your two children possibly earn the deep love that I know you have for them?" he asked, rhetorically.

"They couldn't possibly," she replied.

"Right. And if they could indeed earn it, it wouldn't be love."

Elizabeth nodded emphatically. "When you're right, you're right."

"Here's the fifth thing you can do. When people offer to help, say 'yes' and then tell them how they can help. Don't tell yourself that Solitaire excuse 'I don't want to be a bother.' People love to help and if you don't let them, you are actually depriving them of a chance to feel good about themselves. It's a rip-off to them. Just say 'yes' and everyone wins."

Elizabeth flinched. "I make that mistake all of the time. From now on, when I hear myself telling that lie, I'm going to remind myself of how good I feel when someone asks me for help."

"God bless you. I've always been impressed with your willingness to apply what you've learned."

"Thank you, Dr. Scott."

"You're welcome," he replied.

Then, turning to address the whole group, he said, "And thank you, all of you, for coming today and for being such willing participants. It made the day a lot of fun for me."

SUMMARY OF CHAPTER 9

- In TAG-playing families, people play Team TAG because it allows each participant to not be IT and creates the illusion of being a team—of having a relationship.
- In order to break the game, you need to :

  Think differently–"Here's my chance to have a different sort of conversation."

  Use the "Connect, Then Lead" approach to focus the conversation on someone who is actually a part of the conversation.

  Repeat this approach as often as necessary.

  Make "I statements" such as "Mom, I just want to hear about you, not them."

  If absolutely necessary, end the conversation and give the person another chance the next time you speak with them (and the next, and the next).

- With entire groups who tend to play this game, you might want to develop a closer relationship with one person at a time and then start to slowly expand that circle. Remember not to play Team TAG against the people who are not yet in the circle!
- Remember, also, that you are doing this for them, too. It's the good and the loving thing to do. God IS the connection, which means that everything we do to honor our connections honors our God.
- With other people who play Solitaire, you can:
- Look for what they do right and tell it to them briefly (The 90-10 Rule).

- If, after allowing them time to practice, they still do not receive your compliments and praise, you can let them know (using "I language!") that their refusal to accept your feedback is hurtful to you.

- Make sure to pay attention to them at a time when they are not performing, so they have the opportunity to learn that you love them, not their performance.

- If you play Solitaire, you can change by deciding to pay attention and:

    notice all the greetings and affectionate touch that express people's love and concern for you.

    accept all the compliments they share with you.

    answer the sincere questions they ask you.

    thank them for the gifts they give to you. To be a gracious receiver is an act of love.

    say "yes" to their offers of help to you.

EXERCISE #8

1.) Name a person who frequently tries to involve you in Team TAG and give a recent example. Then, get your mind straight and generate at least three "connect, then lead" responses you could give which would end that game.

2.) Who are the people in your life who are most likely to play Solitaire? What are some of the specific things you could do to help them to see how precious they are to you?

3.) List all of the different ways people tried to tell you today that they loved you or that you mattered to them. What will you need to do differently in order to become a more gracious receiver?

CHAPTER 10:

Moving Beyond the Game: Summary and Planning

"Welcome back. What did you think of the seminar?" asked Dr. Scott.

"It was intensely educational, just like our counseling sessions," said Elizabeth.

Joe agreed. "I learned a lot, for sure."

"I'm glad to hear that. In a minute, I want to hear more about what you learned, as a part of our 'summarize, then strategize' session. First, though, I would like to share with you a summary of my own."

"A summary of what?" Elizabeth wondered.

"Well," replied Dr. Scott, "I have given it a lot of thought and have come up with a way to summarize TAG. Would that be helpful to you?"

Elizabeth and Joe both nodded excitedly.

"For a long time I have been thinking about the reasons why it is of such particular importance to me that Christians, even more so than others, understand and break through the game of TAG.

Then it came to me. It's because the game stands in such contrast with the life we as Christians are called to live. In fact, I have come to think of our faith as the anti-TAG. Or, perhaps, it would be more accurate to call the game the anti-faith.

In order to clarify what I mean, I created a 'compare and contrast' chart that I think summarizes my point very well. When I get done, please let me know what you think. If it seems useful to you, I will start using it with my other clients, as well."

"Okay," Joe smiled. "Let's see what you've got."

"All right," replied Dr. Scott. "It is still a bit rough but here is what I have come up with so far."

TAG	Our Faith
I'm Not Good Enough (NGE) I focus on my 10% (and yours) and am resentful. I believe the serpent; I'm incomplete (Genesis 3:1-5).	**I am a precious child of our God** I see myself through God's eyes; I focus on my 90% (and yours) and am grateful (Psalm 72:14; Isaiah 43:4; Philippians 4:8).
My mistakes "prove" I'm NGE That's why I (and you) deserve to be treated so badly (John 8:5-15) and why I experience shame (Genesis 3:7).	**My mistakes reveal important lessons** We are precious, despite our mistakes; that's why I expect to be treated lovingly and do not judge others (Matthew 7:1; Romans 2:1).
I therefore must hide my mistakes That way, no one will realize that I am NGE and then reject me (Genesis 3:8). I play Frozen TAG and Constant TAG.	**I therefore must embrace my mistakes** That's why I choose to be transparent and accountable; that way I keep growing in faith (Philippians 1:9; I Thessalonians 4:10).
So, I must stay isolated No one can reject me if they don't know the real me (the word "sin" literally means "to be separate") (Luke 15:11-13).	**So that I can live in joyful community** My transparency allows people to know, love, and accept the real me; I experience all forms of right relationship (Luke 15:20-24; Matthew 22:36-40; John 15:12).

When I'm caught, I blame others (Genesis 3:12-13)	**When I'm wrong(ed) I seek to reconcile** (Matthew 5:23-24; Matthew 18:15-18)
I watch for people's mistakes That way, I'm not IT (Mark 3:2).	**I lift people up** That way, they can do God's work (Romans 1:12; I Thessalonians 5:11).
I have no vision for my life That way, I won't look foolish to other people; I maintain my image.	**I actively pursue my vision** That way, my new life helps to usher in the Kingdom (Mark 12:34; Matthew 4:17).
My vision-less life is all about me In my isolation, I try to make sure I get my individual needs met.	**My vision is all about us** Giving is what brings meaning to life. I seek to serve God and others.
My goal is to not get hurt A good day is a day when nothing bad happens to me. On a scale of minus 10 to plus 10, my goal is zero.	**My goal is to have a powerful impact** A good day is a day when miraculously good things happen. My goal is to reach plus 10 every day.

"Does that make sense to you?" he wondered.

"I love it!" exclaimed Elizabeth. "I feel as if I just received a 15-minute summary of our faith and of everything we have learned from you."

Joe nodded. "I feel the same way. That chart is so clear; there is something so helpful about seeing everything laid out that way. Can we have a copy of that?"

"Of course," replied Dr. Scott. "I am honored that you would want one."

Elizabeth smiled and said, "We will put it up on our refrigerator, so that we always will remember what we learned here."

"Great. Speaking of what you learned, weren't the two of you supposed to summarize what you each have learned so far, in our sessions and at the seminar, so that we could devise a 'where do you want to go from here' strategy?"

Joe replied, "I was pleased that you asked us to do that. I always prefer to have a clear plan and I could see that we needed to assess where we were, in order to devise such a plan."

Elizabeth looked a little smug. "Since we knew you were going to ask us that, we each spent some time looking over our notes and we worked as a team to put together a list of the lessons or insights that we found to be most helpful."

Dr. Scott smiled. "You sound pretty pleased with yourself."

Elizabeth replied, "Well, I surely was pleased with the process. Looking over the notes not only helped to prepare me for today's planning session, it also helped me to be aware of the transformation we have experienced already. That makes me feel pretty good about both our present and our future."

"Great. Let's see what the two of you came up with."

Elizabeth showed Dr. Scott their lists and said, "Here are our two summaries, session by session."

<u>Session 1</u>

Joe:

TAG is a destructive game that we all play.

The only goal of the game is to not be wrong (IT).

It will be difficult to motivate myself to work on this relationship, as long as I continue to allow my resentments to blind me to the truth. I need to see Elizabeth through God's eyes. I need to see her for the precious child of God that she is–the wonderful person whose strengths I saw accurately when I first fell in love with her.

The instant I choose to change, the process of change begins.

Elizabeth:

We can choose to quit playing TAG and to improve our relationships today because there is no such thing as "too late."

Although it is tempting to tell ourselves we just want to "coast" for a while, coasting ("the third way") is not actually an option. We are always either getting closer and closer to one another or drifting further and further apart. In truth, coasting is just drifting further apart.

Since that is the case, and since I need to work out my issues with somebody, giving this relationship my best shot right now is the only choice that makes sense.

Session 2

Elizabeth:

It is important to do The Precious Lists daily. We might need to make alternative (Plan B) arrangements some days and we should vary the way we share the lists so we don't get bored or take the process for granted.

Whereas TAG produces great loneliness (me), real life is all about teamwork (us).

TAG-players ask, "Whose fault is it?" But that's a crazy question. Every one of the problems in our marriage is exactly 50-50, since Joe and I have very similar strengths and the flip side of each others' weaknesses.

Joe:

The only thing that kept me trapped in TAG was fear. As soon as I decided to choose love instead of fear, miracles started happening. And those miracles will continue to happen, as long as I don't take them or Elizabeth for granted—as long as I remain grateful.

Dr. Scott has asked us to take a careful look at our unhelpful patterns, not because he wants us to dwell on the past but because he believes that as soon as we understand the pattern perfectly, the solution will become self-evident.

Session 3

Elizabeth:

Getting our relationship right will require, first, that we quit working so hard at doing it wrong. The right way is always the easiest way; we were created by God to be in right relationship with Him and with all of the people in our lives.

God's love binds together all living things. We don't have to force other people to be connected to us; they already are. We need only to acknowledge that sacred connection, honor it, and be grateful for it.

Joe:

Acknowledging our unhealthy patterns helps to eliminate any possible denial.

Acknowledging my half of the pattern keeps me from playing the blame game.

TAG is destructive because:

1.) It leads us to act as if we are alone, which leads to hurtful and ineffective attempts to get our needs met. In reality, we can only get our needs met when we choose to embrace our connections and build intimate relationships with one another.

2.) It leads to boring, repetitive interactions, whereas the love that binds us together creates new possibilities constantly.

3.) It leads us to see ourselves as powerless victims, rather than as the empowered, responsible people that we are.

Our homework assignment is designed to eliminate these three hurtful practices.

Session 4

Joe:

As long as we keep our vision clearly in mind, continue to practice, and focus on what we do right, we will get better–change WILL occur, starting right now. Our God is a God of transformation and that transformational process starts the instant we ask for God's help.

My two most common mistakes were to play Rehearsal and Victim.

Once I saw clearly my half of the patterns and their hurtful effect upon Elizabeth, I was filled with regret, which will powerfully motivate me to do it differently in the future.

Elizabeth:

A mistake cannot be a sign of failure or "proof" that I am a failure, since I am precious. It's just a sign that I need to learn a particular lesson–a lesson that will be very helpful to me.

My two most common mistakes were to play Controller and Attacker.

My 50% of the problem is likely to trigger Joe's, both now and in the future.

If I want transformation to occur, I first must change my thinking (Think-Feel-Do).

Session 5

Joe:

Our marriage can best be understood as an on-going conversation.

The goal of that conversation must be to understand, not to be right.

In TAG, no one tells the truth and no one hears the truth.

The truth is never hurtful, since it is just information about me.

Elizabeth:

An argument is just a sign that no one is listening. It is therefore a waste of time.

To tell the truth requires that I use "I language" to describe my thoughts and emotions, which are more likely to be about what didn't happen (sad) than about what did happen (mad).

To hear the truth requires that I keep my ego out of the conversation and that I focus on offering reassurance, which might involve non-invasive touch, comforting words, the use of "we" language, and offers to help.

If I feel like I'm being attacked, I just say, "I feel like the bad one," which stops the game and uses "I language," which will keep us from playing TAG about playing TAG.

Session 6

Elizabeth:

An argument is just a sign that we are either not telling or not hearing the truth.

We break our patterns by catching ourselves sooner and sooner in the cycle.

The hardest thing for me to do was to tell my truth, instead of judging or controlling others. I will need to keep choosing transparent vulnerability, in order to break my part of the pattern.

Joe:

The hardest thing for me was to hear the truth. I can break this pattern by teasing myself and by remembering how precious Elizabeth is to me.

In life, the process of learning IS the reward.

The four versions of TAG that will be addressed at the seminar are:

Frozen TAG, where we avoid being IT by remaining passive.

Constant TAG, where we avoid being IT by constantly making others IT.

Team TAG, where we both avoid being IT by making a third person IT.

Solitaire, where we avoid having others make us IT by making ourselves IT.

The Morning Seminar

Elizabeth:

Niceness (what you don't do) isn't the same as God's goodness, which is a powerful and active force in its own right. In fact, being nice often prevents us from doing good.

If I feel like Joe is playing Frozen TAG, I can acknowledge my part of the game (control), be clear as to why I want to change my half, practice those reasons, so as to solidify my thinking, refuse to take "no answer" for an answer, let Joe know that I want a closer relationship, and start by freely acknowledging my contributions to the old patterns.

If a group of people are playing Constant TAG, Joe and I can draw upon each other's presence and use the "yes, I see that, too" approach to break the pattern from our end.

Joe:

Two popular myths among Frozen TAG players are: "I'm just protecting you" and "I don't care." Really, we are just protecting ourselves and we always have opinions.

For me to quit playing Frozen TAG, I need to drop those myths, start telling safe people like Elizabeth what I really want, and be accountable to those people. If I wanted to, I also could keep a journal, take a community ed class, continue seeing Dr. Scott, or purchase the materials he has made available to us.

When I am with someone who is playing Constant Tag I can agree with something factual about what they said and then propose a "we" solution.

I also could simply start a related, more positive, conversation.

<u>The Afternoon Seminar</u>

Elizabeth:

When talking to a person who plays Team TAG, I need to change my thinking and then proactively use the "connect, then lead" strategy. I will need to be persistent in this.

If other people in my life play Solitaire, I can help by looking for the 90%, consistently giving brief compliments, and letting them know that I feel hurt when they refuse to accept those compliments. I can also make a point of paying attention to them when they are not performing, through physical affection, listening, soliciting their opinions, and asking them questions.

Joe:

If an entire group plays Team TAG, we can break the game by building relationships with the people in the group, one at a time, while remembering not to play TAG against the people who are not yet in the circle.

As a life-long Solitaire player, I can break the pattern by paying attention to all of the love that I receive, instead of ignoring those messages and striving for approval.

I can start by noticing how happy people are to see me, accepting compliments, answering questions fully, receiving gifts graciously, and allowing others to help me, instead of depriving them of that opportunity.

Elizabeth asked, shyly, "What do you think of our lists?"

Dr. Scott was truly impressed. "Wow, those are great summaries! The two of you really DID put a lot of effort into that!"

"Thank you."

"So, given this great summary of what you've learned and given where you are now, what seems like the next logical step for you?"

Elizabeth answered, "Well, I, for sure, would like to keep coming to you, perhaps once every two or three weeks, so that we keep learning more about TAG–especially how to break it by telling and hearing the truth. I would also like to go to your intensive seminar on intimacy, in order to learn how to take our marriage to a whole new level of closeness and caring. In the meantime, I think we should continue to honor our daily Precious List time, since that has been so important for us.

Joe smiled, nodded his head, and said, "I agree with everything Elizabeth said. I also think we need to keep getting more clarity on The

50-50 Rule and keep getting better at the 'I feel like I'm IT' method of breaking the game. Plus, I would like for us to attend the parenting seminar you mentioned, so that we can teach our kids a whole different set of skills than the ones we learned. And I want to start a small group ministry in my church, to teach other couples the things that we have learned."

Dr. Scott replied, "Those sound like some great ideas. Let's start meeting every other week, instead of every week, and let's also focus on noticing the 50-50 patterns, naming the game when it occurs, and developing the skills necessary to tell and hear the truth. In addition, I would ask that you continue with your daily Precious Time and I'd like to ask for your permission to hold you accountable for the changes you each need to make, if you are to quit playing Frozen TAG and Solitaire. Is that okay?"

Both Joe and Elizabeth nodded their eager assent.

Dr. Scott smiled. "Great. In the meantime, I will have my assistant send you the information on the intimacy and parenting seminars, so that you can register for the dates that work best for you. And, Joe, if you want me to talk with any of the leaders in your church, to help you get that ministry going, I would be glad to do that."

"I'll check into that right away," Joe promised.

"Good. Take care. I look forward to seeing the two of you in a couple of weeks."

EXERCISE #9

It's important that you make a plan for your continued growth, just as Joe and Elizabeth did. That way, all of the changes you have made thus far will be not only preserved but also strengthened.

Please start by reviewing the previous chapter summaries and the various exercises you completed. This will serve to remind you of what you have learned and will clarify for you the work that remains to be done.

What I Have Learned: My Personal Summary

What I've learned about relationships:

Ways I can use what I've learned to help others.

Areas in which I need to continue growing:

The methods or resources I will draw on in order to facilitate that growth:

(note: both of the seminars Joe and Elizabeth mentioned, as well as the set of tapes and CDs Dr. Scott described, are actually available through Beginning Now Ministries. If you are interested in any of those resources, please check out our website at beginningnowministries.org, contact the office at (952) 454-2629, or email the office at dana_LTT@msn.com.).